The Gods of Boxing

A Fighter's View of Boxing from Achilles to Alexander

The Gods of Boxing

Books by James LaFond

The Fighting Edge, 2000
The Logic of Steel, 2001
The First Boxers, 2011
The Gods of Boxing, 2011
All Power Fighting, 2011
When You're Food, 2011
The Lesser Angles of Our Nature, 2012
The Logic of Force, 2012
The Greatest Boxer, 2012
Take Me to Your Breeder, 2014
The Streets Have Eyes, 2014
Panhandler Nation, 2014
The Ghetto Grocer, 2014
American Fist, 2014
Don't Get Boned, 2014
Alienation Nation, 2014
In The Chinks of The Machine, 2014
How the Ghetto Got My Soul, 2014
Saving the World Sucks, 2014
Taboo You, 2014
The Fighting Life, 2014
Narco Night Train, 2014
Into the Mountains of Madness, 2014
Astride the Chariot of Night, 2014
Sacrifix, 2014
Rise, 2014

Motherworld, 2014
Planet Buzzkill, 2014
Fruit of The Deceiver, 2014
Forty Hands of Night, 2014
Black and Pale, 2014
Daughters of Moros, 2014
Fat Girl, 2014
Hurt Stoker, 2014
Poet, 2014
Triumph, 2015
Winter, 2015
The Spiral Case, 2015
Hemavore, with Dominick Mattero, 2015
Yusuf of the Dusk, 2015
Mantid, 2015
RetroGenesis: Day 1, with Erique Watson, 2015
Big Water Blood Song, 2011
Ghosts of the Sunset World, 2011
Beyond the Ember Star, 2012
Comes the Six Winter Night, 2012
Thunder-Boy, 2012
The World is Our Widow, 2013
Behind the Sunset Veil, 2013
Den of The Ender, 2013
God's Picture Maker, 2014
Out of Time, 2015
Seven Moons Deep, 2015

The Gods of Boxing

Copyright James LaFond 2015

Prepared for publication by Jamie King in association with PunchbuggyBooks.

Research Assistant: Erika Cooper, Baltimore County Public Library
Critical Reading: Professor David Carl, Saint John's College at Santa Fe; Jay Harding, Ed.S., University of Iowa, kenpo & kali instructor; Doctor David Lumsden, MMA coach.
Instruction: "Reds" Foley, Ed Jones, "Irish" Johnny Coiley, Arturo Gabriel, Jimmy Hines, Frank Gilbert

This is the second of four volumes that comprise *The Broken Dance: A Fighter's View of Boxing and Prize-fighting from Pre-history to the Fall of Rome.*

The Illustrator

Joseph Bellofatto Junior's paintings and illustrations have been featured on the covers and interiors of *Absolute Magnitude* and *Gateways Magazine*, and books by *Quite Vision Publishing*. He won an honorable mention in the L. Ron Hubbard *Writers Artist of the Future* contest. He lives with his wife, children and dogs in suburban Maryland.

The Author

James LaFond lives and works in the "once great medieval city" of Baltimore Maryland. He has fought 20 submission boxing bouts according to LPR, Gypsy and Greek rules, for 7 wins, 4 losses and 9 draws. James can be reached through the bio page at www.jameslafond.com

For Ted LaFond, who built a gym for an eccentric son.

The Gods of Boxing

Contents

The Illustrator 4
The Author 4
Introduction 9
The Artist's Introduction 9

Chapter 1 11
Boxing with Ghosts 11

Chapter 2 14
The Prize-Fighter's Mind: Understanding the Ancient Boxer's Perspective 14

Chapter 3 17
On the Dug-up 17
    Warrior Excellence 18
    Equipment & Training 19
    Officials 19
    Bout Structure 20
    Rules 21
    Sacred Contests & Prizes 21
    The Life of a Boxer 22

Chapter 4 23
Fists for Thunder-chief 23
    Map 7: Hellas c. 530 B.C. 25

Chapter 5 28
Voices in Stone: Considering Ancient Epitaphs 28
The Plight of Nestor: Aging and Ancient Athletics 31

Chapter 7 34
Fists of Honor: Archaic Boxing from Epeus to Tisander—1220 to 526 B.C. 34
    The Gods of Boxing C. 750 B.C. 37
    Epeus and Euryalus: composed c. 750 B.C. 39
    The Prince, the Adventurer and the Bum 43
    Boxing in 7th Century B.C. Hellas 46

Boxing in Early 6th Century B.C. Hellas 49

Boxing in Mid 6th Century B.C. Hellas: 548-26 B.C. 53

The Tools of the Archaic Boxer...70

An Analysis of Archaic Boxing Techniques in Literature & Art: 750-526 B.C. 77

Strike Type of 48 Strikes 77

Amplification of 48 Strikes..77

Defenses Against 48 Strikes 77

A Stylistic Summary of Archaic Boxing 77

The Cultural Context of Boxing in Archaic Hellas 78

Chapter 8 80

The Air of Agony: A Boxer's View of the 99th Olympiad, 384 B.C. 80

The Two Halves of Humanity: Slavery in Archaic and Classical Hellas 83

Servitude in Classical Hellas 84

Chapter 10 86

Ascension of the Prize-fighter: Deification and the Ancient Athlete 86

Chapter 11 91

Fists of Fame: Classical Boxing from Glaukos to Satyrus, 524 to 325 B.C. 91

Boxing from 520 B.C. to 500 B.C. 93

Boxing From 496 to 485 B.C. 111

5th Century Training and the Psychology of High-handedness 124

Boxing from 484 to 440 B.C. 126

Unsung Boxers c.450 B.C. 130

Boxing From 439 to 412 B.C. 142

Boxing From 411 to 394 B.C. 146

Boxing During the Tenure of Plato: 392 to 351 B.C. 149

Plato on Boxing: Excerpts from Alkibiades II, Gorgias, Republic, Philebus & Laws 150

Boxing during the Tenure of Aristotle: 351 to 325 B.C. 154

Aristotle on Boxing: Excerpts from his Nikomakhaen Ethics 156

Analysis of Classical Boxing Techniques in Literature & Art: 520-336 B.C. ...162

Strike Type of 88 Strikes 162
　　Amplification of 88 Strikes 162
　　Defenses Against 88 strikes 162
　　A Stylistic Summary of Classical Boxing 163
　　The Cultural Context of Boxing in Classical Hellas 163
The Fate of Ancient Boxing 165
　　Boxing Before, During and After Alexander 165
Epilogue: 170
The Life of Boxing to A.D. 551 170
Appendix 173
A Discussion of the Literary Sources 173
　　The Three Layers of Historical Knowledge 173
　　Tertiary Sources 173
　　Secondary Sources 177
　　Primary Sources 177
　　The Author's Reading Method 178
　　Part Two: Select Bibliography of Modern Sources in Order of Importance 178
　　Select Bibliography of Ancient Sources in Chronological Order 182

The Gods of Boxing

Introduction

"...Pugilism is of ancient date in reference to the Greeks and Romans, and that it was sanctioned by these distinguished nations, in their public sports, and in the education of youth, to manifest its utility in strengthening the body, dissipating all fear, and infusing a manly courage into the system."
    -Pierce Egan, *Boxiana I*

...This is a book about warriors; about fighters, as well as about the men and women who are both fascinated by them and who condemn them. LaFond's book is the most impressive attempt to understand this dual reaction of fascination and condemnation in the face of violence that I have ever read. Informed by his painstaking research work in the library as well as through no doubt even more painful firsthand experience, LaFond brings a unique perspective to a complex body of information. In equal parts an impressive work of rigorous scholarship, insightful psychology, and provocative philosophy, this book is a rare example of the kind of perceptive and engaging history too often buried under the weight of overly zealous but narrow-minded academic research.

LaFond writes like an angel with a razor—he is careful and precise, but with a light touch and an accurate eye for what will entertain and delight as well as inform and enlighten.

    -Professor David Carl, Saint John's College at Santa Fe

The Artist's Introduction

From the artist's stand point, illustrating non-fiction is more demanding than fiction. While it shares many aspects of traditional illustration it places great limitations on the application of the artist's imagination. Most non-fiction—especially books of historical scope—come with its own stock imagery. The subject matter of this book is no different.

Attacking the illustration for this book not only required the setting aside of stereotypical images of the era, it demanded understanding the context in which the art was created and the purpose it [the actual artifact] served. Much of the art that survives goes beyond the aesthetic, and serves a function of utility like the illustrations in this book. When evaluating the art for reproduction, examining the original work up close was necessary;

viewing the numerous archives of photo reproduction used by historians was simply not adequate.

    Just as much of human knowledge has evolved over the centuries, so has art. Each generation discovers some new method, means of observation, and enhancement of craftsmanship for the purpose of rendering the natural world with greater accuracy and conveying the human condition through various media. When starting work on this project I expected to see a certain crudity in technique given the age of the images. Much to my delight, I found the opposite to be true. Upon actually inspecting these objects I immediately felt the thrill the artisan must have felt during the actual crafting of the work, even though the artist lived in a vastly different time and culture. I can only hope that the works created within this book—both reproductions and original art—are able to convey the craftsmanship and stand the test of time endured by the original art.

Chapter 1
Boxing with Ghosts

"Over the dead one are lit
 Some silent stars."
  -Dag Hammarskjold, *Markings*

    In preparing the text I have made every effort to permit the ancients to speak for themselves through their preserved words and images. However, owing to the patchwork record left us, portions of this work have fallen to my interpretation.

    For the interpretation of actual fighting methods I have trusted first to my own experience as a fighter and coach; second to the deductions of those fighters and coaches I hold in high regard; and third—where my experience and advisors have been insufficient—to fighting [not sparring] under the conditions and rules known to have been current during the period under examination.

    For the interpretation of the social contexts within which the fighters pursued their arts I have consulted the published works of the most respected academics in the field in question. Where contradictions have arisen I have generally sided with the most recent scholarship. In cases where theories need be advanced based on multidisciplinary sourcing of my own, or where I am in disagreement with the academic consensus, I have made plain my divergence from accepted opinion. For those interested in comparing the material presented herein with the works of other modern sources, you may wish to read the Appendix before the next chapter.

    Ancient quotes, have, in most cases, been adapted from the Greek from two or more published translations, supplemented by my own study of the ancient dialects of this language. In some cases, such as epigrams translated in the late 19th and early 20th Centuries [When translators often mangled the subject in order to flex their own poetic muscles in English.], I have translated these pieces on my own [These will be the ugly sounding ones.] with intentional bluntness. Homer's extensive verse descriptions of prize-fights in the *Iliad* and *Odyssey* are presented in narrative prose.

The Gods of Boxing

The captions accompanying the illustrator's reproductions of ancient art, as well as his original pieces based on my notes, are generally extensive, and are, in actuality, discussions that attempt to address the social and biomechanical aspects of the illustration. The most interesting thing about this study is the nature of the surviving art. Almost all of it appears either (1.) on prize jugs for the storage of [very expensive] olive oil, which were actually trophies for the victor, or (2.) on tableware. Imagine a world that was so obsessed with the fighting arts that your plates, cups, bowls and salad dressing bottles would be decorated with scenes of boxing and MMA, both bouts and training!

The vast majority of the information contained in this book appears in Chapters 7 & 11. This material is arranged in strict chronological order. The other chapters are actually brief contextual pieces that were originally composed as side bars for what had been a massive book. From 2000 thru 2005 I reduced the original outline of my comprehensive study of ancient boxing and prizefighting [originally intended to cover all boxing up to 2000] 27 times. Eventually, in 2005 I made the final format change, and decided to abbreviate the study at the Death of Alexander, as the nature of the social context and source material changed drastically at this time. The material in this volume represents the high point of boxing in ancient Hellas, but encompasses only a brief interlude in the history of ancient boxing. Please keep in mind, as you discover these ancient fighters, that they were the inheritors of a vast combative tradition, and that they would bequeath a legacy of sacral submission combat to be practiced by hundreds of generations of Olympians to come.

Although this book has been written for the active fighter it is also intended to be a reliable resource for the student of history. It is my sincere hope that I have not compromised or distorted the legacy of the ancient fighters whose lives I have sought to illuminate for their descendants, nor compromised the standards of inquiry first pioneered by the Athenian historian [inquirer] Thukydides in 404 B. C. It is my intention that this book be enjoyed equally by those whose actions are too rarely credited with wisdom, and those whose wisdom all too often fails to escape the prison of thought.

It may be of some interest to the reader that the city that produced most of the surviving boxing art during this period, Athens, may be translated as Thought-town. In fact, the modern word academy derives from the Hellenic Akademy, which was an Athenian athletic facility that doubled as a university. While we are discussing translations, I should note that I have utilized K rather than the Latin-inspired C in the spelling of most Hellenic places, names and terms. [There was no C in the Hellenik alphabet. This surely seems like a little thing to quip about. But it is another small reminder of how our view of the Hellenes of 2,500 years ago has been distorted through the prism of the Hellenized Romans of 1,800 years ago.] This is in line with some current trends in scholarship, but may seem odd to the reader; Achilles is the exception, since he's on the cover. I'll spell his name like I'm a Roman so as not to drive my editor up the wall and to keep the text consistent with the cover.

Illustrations: Joseph did 112 numbered illustrations for this study, 9 amplification illustrations, 17 posture sketches, and 8 maps. That is 146 works of art, researched and worked-up by hand. This was a two-man project. Although the original work has now been broken down into 4 volumes, I have retained the original numbering system. Below is the art catalog for the entire study, which I have titled *The Broken Dance.*

Volume One—*The First Boxers*: Sketches A-Q, Figures 1-23; Maps 1-6

Volume Two—*The Gods of Boxing*: Figures 32-49, 52-91, 111; Maps 7-8

Volume Three—*All-Power-Fighting*: Figures 24-31, 50-51, 92-110; Maps 7-8

Volume Four—*The Boxer Dread*: Figure 112 [The nature of the extant art for this period is drastically different and less abundant, and, as of this writing, it has not been determined how it shall be represented in this volume.] Maps 7-8

I am pleased with the exposition of core Western martial arts that Joseph and I have achieved in this volume, and I hope the reader is as amazed at the accomplishments of these ancient fighters as I was, when first I saw them as they saw themselves.

-James LaFond, September 6th, 2010, Baltimore Maryland

Chapter 2
The Prize-Fighter's Mind: Understanding the Ancient Boxer's Perspective

"Boxing is a very jealous sport."

-Chris Arreola, heavyweight contender, 8/13/2010

When considering the subject of ancient boxing it might be helpful to use two modern practices as vantage points for our study. The first perspective is that of the modern self-defense practitioner, whose art likely echoes some of the mechanics of ancient boxing. The second perspective is that of the modern boxer or MMA fighter, whose quest, if not his methods, echoes that of his ancient counterpart. Of the two, the self-defense practitioner is going to be more likely to access a book such as this, as self-defense arts tend to be curriculum-based, while prize-fighting tends to be more of a craft, featuring more oral transmission.

It will be most useful to contrast self-defense and prize-fighting at this point so that the various misconceptions self-defense practitioners might harbor concerning prize-fighting may be excluded from our interpretation. It is this author's opinion that the study of ancient boxing is the perfect place to achieve a synergy between self-defense and prize-fighting. The emerging modern sport of MMA; based on self-defense and prize-fighting, and focused as it is on evolution, offers an excellent model for the understanding of ancient boxing that I have sought to achieve through this study.

Despite the fact that modern gloved boxing is touted as a self-defense art and that its methods are often used by self-defense enthusiasts; boxing, and other prize-fighting arts are not exercises in self-defense, but distillations of ritual warfare. While self-defense arts are actually systems for acquiring and applying functional defense skills replete with formalized curricula, instruction and testing; prize-fighting arts are simply formats for pitting combatants against one another for the sake of cultivating and displaying those attributes traditionally useful in war: courage; tenacity; strength; speed; stamina; etc.

The Gods of Boxing

The fact that some prize-fighting methods from boxing, and other arts such as Muay Thai, Wrestling and Brazilian Jiu Jitsu, do have functional self-defense applications, and that people such as myself have mined these arts for just such applications, has clouded the picture of prize-fighting for the modern student of the fighting arts.

While self-defense is traditionally a skill-based endeavor, with most systems featuring between 50 and 150 specified techniques; prize-fighting is an attribute-based pursuit that requires a higher conditioning base-line for competition than its skill base-line. For example: most amateur boxers, upon entering competition, only possess 1 generalized defensive technique [the guard] and 2 specific offensive techniques [jab, straight right]. However the conditioning level of these athletes in terms of [courage, stamina, tenacity] is far beyond that demonstrated by a typical karate black belt, who will possess dozens of tested skills. Every black belt must be able to demonstrate their art's skill-set on demand.

A professional boxer, however, may fight successfully for decades with only two or three effective punches and as many defenses. Donovan "Razor" Rudick terrorized the heavyweight ranks in the 1990's as a converted one-armed southpaw, due to injury.

The gulf between prize-fighters and self-defense practitioners is greater than is usually recognized. Such basic terms as sparring and fighting typically have a different meaning.

Sparring among self-defense practitioners is regarded as a test, to demonstrate mastery of skill application. Sparring among boxers is just practice-fighting. Prize-fights are fought, not to demonstrate skill, but to establish and reward dominance according to an often brutal set of parameters. These contests can, and do, reward the naturally tougher, more conditioned, or more gifted athlete, more often than the more clinically skilled athlete. In light of these facts, the self-defense practitioner who examines the methods of the ancient boxer should be mindful of the narrowly brutal context in which prize-fights were—and continue to be—fought.

The modern boxer, coach or enthusiast that examines the material within this book might be led, by his or her experience, to make misinterpretations of their own. In the history of the inquiry into ancient boxing this has often been the case. The modern boxer, teacher or viewer must not look at the techniques of the ancients and see an art that only matured in modern times. Modern boxing owes its origin to the inspiration provided by the ancient boxers. However it is not a technical evolution of ancient boxing. Modern boxing is at once an evolution of gloved sparring, and a devolution of bare-knuckle fighting. The boxers of ancient Greece fought with hand-gear that spawned gauntlet boxing, and was more compatible with ancient MMA [pankration or all-power-fighting] than modern boxing is with modern MMA.

We would do well to remember that boxing in the ancient world was much tougher than it is in the modern world. When considering these fighters of the past keep in mind that they fought without the benefit of weight-classes, rounds, 10-counts, clinches, shoes or even gloves, and that some of the blows that modern boxers rely on to win by knockout were more difficult—or even hazardous—to deliver without the benefit of advanced hand protection. As brutal as modern boxing is, roughly two-thirds of all pro bouts go the distance. The ancients fought to the finish every single time.

The word athlete is key to understanding prize-fighting. This is an ancient Greek term which means prize-seeker. Another word, agony, is important to understanding the ancient and modern prize-fighter. Agony is the ancient Greek term for the trials of training. The term for training, or contest-preparation, was agonistics. When considering the men who boxed in the times of Achilles, Leonidas and Alexander, one should be respectful of the extreme hazards and grueling trials that faced those who contended in a ritual that could—and did—elevate a select few to the status of king, hero, or even a god.

Chapter 3
On the Dug-up

"History does not write its lines except in blood."

-Shaykh Abdulla Azzam

    There was no ancient boxing ring: no cage; no octagon; no mat. The Hellenic term was skamma, which literally meant "the dug-up". This was a turned patch of earth on the race-course. An area would be pick-axed and cleared of stones and manure, and used for the "heavy events" or combat sports of pale: "hand-struggling" or "wrestling"; pugmakhia "fist-fighting" or "boxing"; and pankration "all-power-thing" or "MMA".
    Every boy that took up boxing—and every boy did—had already put in years on the dug-up as a wrestler, and had done his share of running, jumping, stone-throwing, and javelin-throwing on the un-raked course, so there was no question that his feet were tough enough. Boxing instruction typically began at 12-years-old. By age 16, the boy may have chosen to compete as a pankratiast "all-power-fighter" particularly if he excelled at wrestling and boxing. With the exception of Sparta, MMA does not appear to have been mandatory for boys.
    The dug-up itself would be picked and raked by the younger fighters as part of their conditioning. A good modern analogy to this fighting surface would be to take a heavy rake to the second-base area of a base-ball diamond. Continuous raking for a few hours by one man will develop a 16 to 20 foot circle of soft powdered dirt about two inches deep. The feel is much different than sand. As soon as you begin to shadow box you will experience a boxer's joy. This provides the best boxing footing imaginable. You can slide as easily as if you were on wax tile—if you wish. The powder will cushion your feet like insoles. The hard earth beneath can be gripped by your toes and the balls of your feet—with the dirt acting as traction powder—as easily as the best boxing or wrestling shoes can grip a dry rough ring canvas. The dug-up with a few inches of powder does not favor the boxer or the puncher. Politics, though, might intrude.

The Gods of Boxing

What if Milo [*Sheep*] of Kroton was going to be wrestling on the dug-up before the boxers came out? Milo was the most dominant wrestler of all time, and a man could be killed getting slammed onto a shallow boxers' dug-up. What if the local priests of Hermes, not wanting the hometown wrestlers to have their bodies wrecked being slammed to the dug-up by Milo, opted for a deep dug-up; perhaps a hand's depth worth of powder? What effect would this have on the boxers? A deep dug-up would slow down the boxer and lighten the puncher's blows, tiring both of them. This would tend to turn the boxing matches into a battle of attrition. For the boxer it would be like having a deep-tissue massage before fighting. For a puncher it would be like fighting on one of those cheap plastic ring covers.

There was another factor, the size of the dug-up. Dominant MMA fighters would want a small dug-up, since their event could be won be pushing their man out, or getting him to step out of the dug-up, therefore submitting before the gods. There is ample evidence that boxers were forced to stay in by their seconds and the local officials. The typical dug-up was circular and about as wide as a modern boxing ring, from 16-feet to 24 feet. Again, politics, tradition and even the size or reputation of a certain attending athlete could be a key factor in determining the dimensions of the dug-up.

Warrior Excellence

Every free man in Greece during this period became involved in boxing as part of a decade-long mixed martial arts program. This program was in place in every Greek-speaking community in order to develop arête, or warrior-excellence. This single word has been the subject of at least one entire book. It was a holistic concept of warrior virtues that extended to civics, religion, intellectual life, and the martial arts. Every citizen, whether he was destined to be a potter, philosopher or mercenary captain, aspired to these qualities as a prerequisite for manhood and citizenship.

Of the many virtues that comprised warrior-excellence courage was foremost, and boxing was used to develop this aspect of the warrior. The entire fitness program comprised: running; jumping; javelin-throwing; stone-throwing; wrestling; boxing; MMA; and, for those who could afford the equipment, heavy-infantry or cavalry drill.

The Gods of Boxing

Equipment & Training

Boxing was one of the gymnastic, or "naked" arts, practiced in the gymnasium. On the grounds of the gymnasium, which was an open-air facility, would be a palaestra or "hand-struggling-ground" or "wrestling-ground". This facility was named after Palaestra, the lesser goddess of wrestling, who was the daughter of the god Hermes. Hermes was the god of contests, travelers—all top athletes were big travelers—and escort of souls. This was his temple. It also doubled as an MMA school, a men's club, a boy's club, and store house. The wrestling-ground will be discussed in detail in Chapter 8.

Equipment provided for the boxer at the wrestling-ground, by the community, included a pick for preparing the dug-up, olive oil for protecting the skin, and water. He would provide his own barely cakes, hand-straps, scraper [for cleaning off the oil and dirt] and his penis string. This equipment will be discussed in detail in Chapters 7 and 11.

Officials

Officials at agons or "contests" were known as rod-bearers. These men were all priests of the god presiding over the contest. The priests of Hermes would officiate over all civic contests. Even these, while not dedicated to a specific god, or hero [saint], were sacral events. We cannot really use the word secular to describe any aspect of ancient Hellenic life. There's was an intensely religious culture. At panHellenic "all-Greek" contests, which were dedicated to a particular god, the priests of that god would officiate. One can imagine though, that the priests of Hermes would be present in a supporting role.

We can only guess at how the priests organized themselves as rod-bearers to oversee the contests. But we are familiar with the rod-bearer's appearance and function. He is always depicted as a tall man in middle years, indicating that he was probably a high-level athlete in his youth. He wore a purple robe that was draped over his left shoulder, hung just past the knees, and did not drag on the ground. Purple was a sacred color, worn by kings, rod-bearers and other officials. The rod-bearer, of course, carried a rod: a 4 to 5 foot long thumb-thick staff of flexible wood, like willow. The stick was sometimes forked into two points at one end. This tool could be used to point out something, separate fighters, keep fighters in the dug-up, and, most importantly, to beat the fighters.

Rod-bearers doubled as trainers, and, before a big contest, fighters might have to train under their scrutiny before being allowed to compete. In such cases the rod might also be used to prod, punish or instruct the fighter. During actual competition the rod would be used to enforce the rules. A fighter who was caught breaking a rule would be beaten with the rod until he stopped breaking the rule. No break was called to enforce this discipline. If a fighter was caught clinching he would be beaten until he let go. If he gouged an opponent he might be beaten until the other fighter recovered.

Rod-bearers were also charged with supervising the drawing of lots, and disqualifying and/or fining fighters who had demonstrated unsportsmanlike conduct or were judged guilty of offending the god of the contest. These men had more in common with a Marine Corp drill instructor than a modern referee.

Bout Structure

Fighters who were deemed by the rod-bearers fit enough to compete in a contest would draw lots. An odd number of contestants would result in a bye. The modern concept that this was unfair did not apply. The goddess Fortune got her say at this time.

Pairs of matching lots marked with the letters of the Greek alphabet were placed in a helmet. After the helmet was shaken fighters would draw their lots and be assigned to fight the fighter who held their matching lot. Fights were probably arranged in alphabetical order. Fighters often fought to the tune of a piper playing the double-flute.

All bouts consisted of a single round. There is some evidence from the time just after the period under study [212 B.C.] that fighters in the final round might agree to a single rest break during their bout. There is no evidence for rest breaks before or after that date.

A bout ended in one of three ways: submission; knockout; or disqualification. The events were single-elimination contests.

The Gods of Boxing

Rules

There were 4 fouls in Hellenic boxing: kicking; clinching; biting; and gouging. Anything else went. Although a fighter could not dig at the eye or other parts with his fingers he was permitted to spear or poke another fighter in the eyes. No targets were off limits: one could strike the throat; spine; back of the head; kidneys; and even the groin. A fighter could also stand over a fallen opponent Dempsey-style and beat him where he sat, or as he tried to rise. There were no rules against head-butting or elbowing. It may be that some contests had their own specific rules and conventions enforced by their priests.

While these rules may seem unnecessarily brutal to the modern fighter, there were two practices that insured that these bouts did not degenerate into death-matches. First, fighters were permitted to submit verbally, or by raising a finger, which often occurred after a fighter had been knocked down. A fighter's trainer [usually his father or brother] was also permitted to stop the fight to save his fighter. [There is only slim evidence for this, so it would be unusual.] Finally, any fighter who killed his opponent, even if by accident, was disqualified, fined, and barred from future entry into that contest; the implication being that a fighter was responsible for preserving the life of his opponents.

Sacred Contests & Prizes

Each town or city would have its own local annual contest. The prizes for these third-tier events are unknown. In late antiquity they would sometimes pay big money.

The second-tier events were held at larger towns and cities in honor of a bewildering variety of deities. The most prominent of these would be the PanAthenaea contest at Athens, held every 4 years, in honor of the city's patron goddess Athena. The prizes were large jugs of olive oil—essentially money in liquid form. Another was the Heraea contest, held at Argos every 4 years, in honor of the goddess Hera. A shield was given as a prize. That would be like winning a Kevlar vest in modern terms. The gods most often honored with contests by the lesser cities and towns were, listed in order of frequency: Apollo, the sun, god of excellence, and boxing; Zeus, chief of the gods; Poseidon, god of the sea, breaker of horses; and Athena, goddess of wisdom. There were many other gods.

The Gods of Boxing

The first-tier events were the contests of the **period**. The period games consisted of: The Olympia, held every 4 years in August, in honor of Zeus, at the holy precinct of Olympia near the town of Elis, the prize being an olive wreath; the Pythia, held every 4 years in July, in honor of Apollo, at the holy city of Delphi, for a wreath of bay; The Isthmian [*Land-bridge*], held every 2nd odd year in April, in honor of Poseidon, at the great city of Korinth [think Los Angeles], for a pine branch; and the Nemean, held every 2nd odd year in July, in honor of Zeus, at the small town of Nemea, for a wreath of parsley. The Olympia and Pythia did not happen on the same year. The period contests did not give cash prizes, although there judges might levy cash fines. An athlete competed in these contests for honor: for himself; his family; and his home town. A fighter who won a victory at a period game would be given free eating privileges at the local mess hall for life, and might be voted a pension, especially for an Olympic victory.

There were no second or third-place finishers, just the victor and those he defeated. After the contest every fighter would take part in the great feast put on by the priests. Only the victor earned the right to the real prize, which was the opportunity to hire a sculpture to make a likeness of him and carve a victory plaque at his feet, listing his name, his father, home town, and his achievements. These men fought for immortality.

The Life of a Boxer

Sports in the ancient world were not professional careers in the modern sense. It was more a kin to a brutal period of scholastic sports in which only the very best received any material compensation. The fame, however, was far greater for a boxer or any of the other athletes, then for their modern counterparts. Consider a world without ball sports: no NFL, NBA, MLB, NHL, soccer, rugby, extreme sports, etc. The ancient concept of an athlete was of an individual. The only sports were combat and track and field.

While athletes who won the five-exercises [track & field] and MMA often went on to become military and political leaders, boxers tended to return to a lower profile life. The most important thing for a modern fighter to realize about life as an ancient fighter was that the man was not defined by his sport, but by his victories. Remember, every man was a wrestler, and every man a boxer. Tisander of Naxos was not remembered as Tisander the Boxer, but as Tisander of Naxos, who won 4 contests at Olympia in boxing. And, as for the champion boxer, more so than for any other athlete, the true prize was not won until after he had passed from life.

Chapter 4
Fists for Thunder-chief

A Fighter's view of Boxing at the 13th Nemean Agon, 547 B.C.

Crest approached the dug-up with confidence, and gazed across the freshly raked circle in contempt. He was being called the Lion of the Argives for having survived the Battle of Three Hundred Duels against the Men of the Silent Land, and for his crushing victory with the fist at The Healer's Contest. The local trainer that father had hired to prepare him for the agonies of this contest had warned him that he would be facing a higher level of competition, as men came far from overseas to test themselves on the very ground where Thunder-chief's mighty son had strangled the Nemean Lion in antiquity.

The scrawny islander—some oarsman off an Asian ship—facing him from across the dug-up would be his first sacrifice to Thunder-chief. He was worried about the tall man from Rope who had drawn the flat-faced old fist-fighter from Tower-hill for the second bout. But the little man he faced now did not worry him much. He was not even a heavy-armed fighter, but a sailor, a stone-thrower at best.

The rod-bearer struck the hard earth beyond the dug-up with the butt of his long hard stick and the piper took up the fist-song. Crest walked in behind a high two-fisted guard. The islander circled to Crest's left, menacing him with a quick sneaky jab. Crest jabbed as he stepped left and then shifted two a right lead as he came down with his powerful hammer-fist. No contact. The thin man had slipped and side-stepped to Crest's left. His trainer spoke from the sideline, "Wear him down boy. Take your time."

The dug-up had been raked to a fine powder to the depth of his longest finger. His trainer had been satisfied that the dug-up would favor Crest, him being the largest of the fist-fighters and having good strong legs. He would just have to be patient, and let the islander slow down.

He continued to step with his jab, but had to stop shifting to a right lead when he chopped down with his right. Every time he shifted the little man stepped around to Crest's right and stabbed at his eyes with his fingertips. He had missed the eyes. But Crest's face was torn and bleeding from these raking attacks, and blood from his eye-brow was beginning to seep into his eye. His trainer yelled, "Jab, boy, jab!"

The Gods of Boxing

Crest snapped out a jab and his ears rang and jaw ached as a hard fist smashed him in the chin. He had not even seen it coming. He stepped and jabbed again, catching the man on the forehead, only to eat a counter-punch that smashed his lips. He could taste blood and brought his hammer fist down without shifting, only to have the little man step out from underneath the blow and pop up with a combination of short punches that stung his right cheek and numbed his eye. His trainer barked, "Thump the ribs and cuff the ears before the damned hare blinds you! Punish him—step on his feet!"

Crest extended his lead and stalked the man. As the islander stepped right to get around Crest's extended lead, the big man hooked a slap to his ear. The islander read the hook and hooked him in the bicep with his fist and stepped to the outside and sunk a hammer-fist into his left kidney. Crest groaned and clinched, under-hooking the smaller man. As he attempted to spin away from the road-bearer who was closing in, he noticed, for the first time, the opponent's trainer: an old one-eyed man with a broken nose and swollen ears, rocking on his heels at the edge of the dug-up, giving cryptic advice in an odd dialect, with a soft grandfatherly voice. He suddenly felt like he was a lone shield man facing a horseman and a *stone-thrower* on the battlefield. His trainer was yelling, "Break and hammer boy!"

As the rod-bearer began to slash into his broad back with the wicked rod of twisted willow, the piper slowed to a shrill haunting cadence—cruelly slapping the hard packed earth with his sandaled feet, dancing like some evil nymph before the smoking altar above the dug-up. As crest sought to push off, the islander slipped between his hands and brought his small hard skull up into Crest's chin, slamming his teeth together right through the tip of his tongue, which fell to the earth as his mouth filled with warm blood. The rod stopped ripping into his back, but he could feel the earth under his knees and a rush of nausea as his left ear rang from a punch and his nose snapped, showering his chest with blood. The world spun to the shrill frantic cadence of the mad piper…

The cruel piper had ceased his taunting tune. He heard vaguely familiar voices speak words that he could not comprehend. A rush of warmth, at once a chill and an awakening, flowed up his neck into his head. He felt strong hands holding up his head, as other hands cautiously relieved his left leg from the twisted position under his body that was causing the ache in his knee. The rays of the Archer stung his eyes as they were washed clear of blood. His father and trainer heaved him to his feet and drug him between them from the dug-up.

The Gods of Boxing

As they seated him on a small folding stool his eyes were drawn to the altar of Thunder-chief. He then came slowly to the realization that he had been sacrificed to the chief of gods by the fists of the islander as surely as a lumbering ox by the ax of a priest.

He was overcome with guilt. "Father, I have disgraced you. I have disgraced our people."

The trainer cut off his father before he could respond, "Nonsense, boy. You were brave—didn't submit. We had to dig you out of the dug-up ourselves. Just sit and watch—you'll see. There'll be five rounds of fist-fighting today. This little bastard is going to be scattering teeth before the altar all afternoon—I can't wait to see him pound the snot out of that war-criminal from Rope. Better to be the first lamb led to the altar, than to be last, knowing full-well what Fortune has waiting under her skirt."

The priest had just returned from throwing the tip of Crest's tongue on the altar fire. The Man of the Silent Land from Rope was advancing onto the dug-up across from the flat-faced old man from Tower-hill. The rod-bearer struck the hallowed ground with the butt of his staff, the tip of which was stained darkly with Crest's own blood. The piper took up the fist-song once again, and, just like that, like the passing of a day into night, Crest was forgotten. Only one man would be remembered for fist-fighting on this day, and it would not be him.

Map 7: Hellas c. 530 B.C.

Cities and towns are indicated by a dark circle.
Major athletic centers are indicated by dark squares.
Home towns of famous boxers are indicated by hollow circles.
Home towns of famous all-power-fighters are indicated by a hollow circle with a dot in the center.
This map was prepared by Joseph based on a hand-drawn original provided by the author. There are some distortions in the interiors of the larger land masses.

Hellas

Magna Greacia

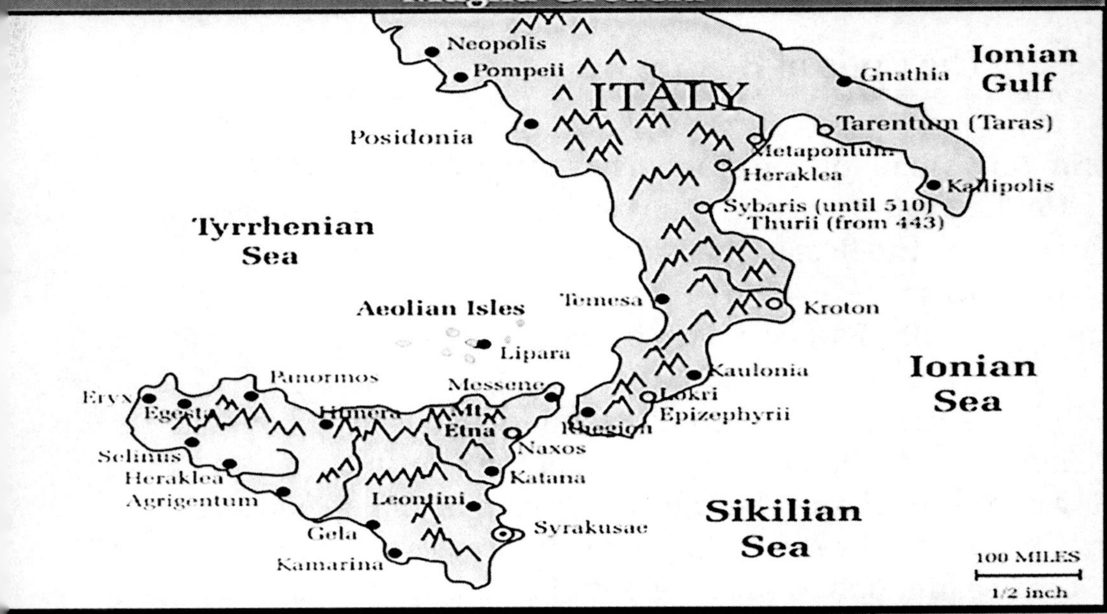

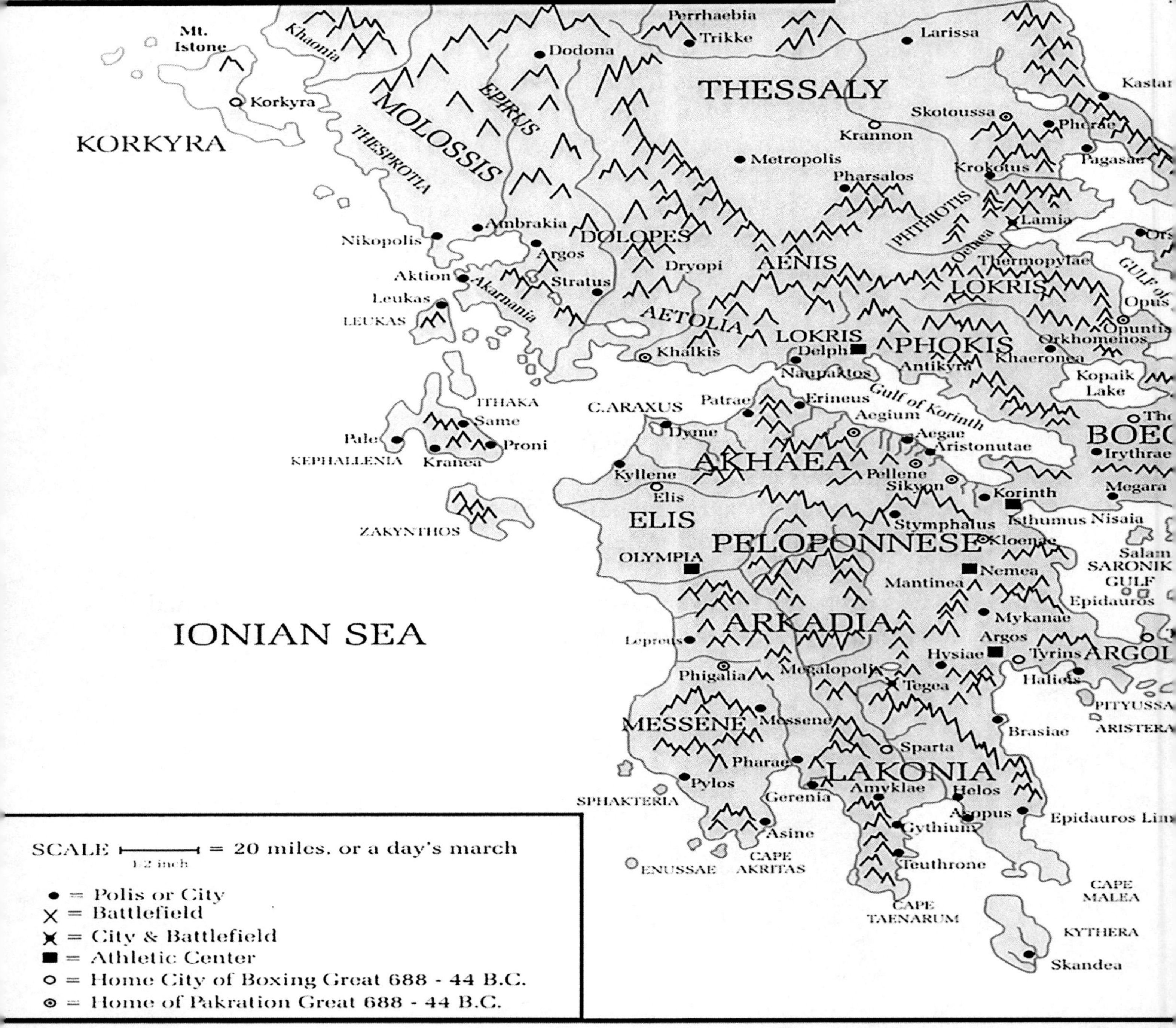

c. 530 B.C.

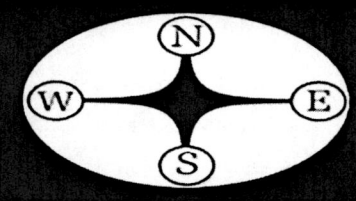

Chapter 5
Voices in Stone: Considering Ancient Epitaphs

"Epitaphs were opportunities for the dead to pass on messages, threats, warnings or advice to future generations."
        -Professor David Carl

Most of the information we possess about fighters from the ancient period was provided at the expense of the fighter and/or his family or community. Unlike the great prehistoric war chief Achilles, whose heroic identity would gain imperishable status thanks to Homer, the athlete of antiquity typically made arrangements for his own immortality.

Once a fighter's statue had been sanctioned by the priestly caretakers of a sacred precinct [such as the Altis at Olympia] where his statue would be raised, he or his family or descendents [in the case of posthumous monuments such as those dedicated to Agias and Polydamas in the 4th Century B.C.] would then hire the necessary craftsmen, including a poet to compose the lines.

The substance of athletic epitaphs are our best guide to the ultimate concerns of the prize-fighter himself. The elements of the athletic epitaph of the Archaic and Classical periods fall into two broad categories: requisite information distinguishing the victor, that is always present and forms the core of the epitaph; and additional information meant to differentiate the victor.

The required elements of a victor's epitaph, which were often etched on the base of his life-sized victory statue, remain simple and modest compared to the boasts of the athletes of late antiquity and the biographies of modern champions. The constant elements of this formula reflect the social conventions of the day that in a traditional society, were surely shared by the majority of athletes. Of primary importance was the victor's home town. Second in importance was his name, which, in many cases seems to have been a fight name earned in sport or war. Third were the sacred contest, sport, and age-grade in which the victory or victories commemorated on the statue were won. These three constants provided the fighter with a clear indication of his agonistic duty: to honor his community by the pursuit of victory in a sacred contest against worthy rivals.

There are six additional elements appearing on or accompanying athletic epitaphs, that, given their frequency, indicate those aspects of achievement that the fighters' themselves yearned to have preserved for posterity. The most important and personal of these was recognition of the fighter's father. Virtually all epitaphs name the father of the victor, whether his victory had been gained as a boy, youth or adult.

The preponderance of paternal recognition along with the near total absence of recognition for the trainer of a victor indicates that the Hellenes were believers in genetic pre-disposition for athletic success, and that many fighters were trained by their fathers. Support for the father-as-trainer theory—so unusual in modern times—can be found in the story of Glaukos, the practice of having the fathers and brothers of a contestant swear an oath alongside him that he had trained faithfully for the fight, and the presence of numerous athletic dynasties as indicated by the extant victory lists found in Pausanias and Pindar.

The second most frequent boast of a victor was the name of the sculpture who crafted his statue. This would even extend to crediting the school, home-town or the teacher of the sculpture.

The third most frequent subject of a victor's statue would be his military service. Although all athletes served in their community's—usually modest—military establishment, those who won duels, commanded troops, fought in the front rank, distinguished themselves in combat, and/or died in battle, had these honors inscribed on their victory plaque. Those modern historians who insist that the military-athletic relationship in Archaic and Classical times was minimal, should consider the fact that a claim to distinguished military service was one of the most coveted boasts a victorious athlete could make when he finally, with the aid of priest, poet and sculpture, staked his claim to immortality.

One of the two minor types of claims made by athletes on victory plaques were claims to extracurricular feats such as strong man stunts. The other unusual claim was the fighter's ethnicity. Some fighters paid to have their tribal or clan affiliation noted [many communities being a collection of various tribes and clans.] By classical times only the Athenians and Eleans seemed to care about one's tribal heritage, a claim that was losing relevance even in the fractious city of Athens. One rare athletic claim that was sometimes made was "winning without a bye". This was considered a notable achievement in a single-elimination event.

In order to understand the value attached to fame, which is essentially an information-based form of immortality, one must appreciate the fact that the ancient Hellenes had no heaven to look forward to. The dead, even great Achilles, descended into shadow, to the cities of dust, to mourn their life past. A victor though, could be remembered as he was in his prime for generations after his last grandchild had passed. Furthermore, a victor who was either blessed or cursed could become a hero [ghost/saint], and receive offerings from the living, and, even better, be given the opportunity to interceded [on a very limited basis] on behalf of mankind, from the world of perpetual gloom believed to exist beyond the world of the living. [One could earn, through virtue in life, a better place in Hades.]

Most importantly of all, a hero, who is sufficiently revered and solicited for blessings often enough, might attain the status of a god, and ultimately escape the gloomy abode of the dead for the mythical realm of Olympus. The boxers of antiquity knew from their studies and the stories of their grandfathers, that Herakles and Polydeukes were famed warriors and combat athletes who had transcended life to be counted among the gods. It was no accident, that every athlete that came to be worshipped as a hero had been a boxer or MMA fighter, and that the only type of athlete regarded as having a chance at reach god status was the boxer. [For a detailed discussion of deification see Chapter 10.]

Regardless of a fighter's hopes or chances for immortality as a victor, a meaningful afterlife as a hero, or everlasting life [not the cozy Christian ideal, but more like the tortured angst of a modern gothic vampire] as a minor god, it all began with his epitaph etched in stone at the base of his victory statue.

Chapter 6
The Plight of Nestor: Aging and Ancient Athletics

"My legs no longer steady, friend, dead on my feet,
  nor do my arms shoot from the shoulder—
  stunning punches, the left and right are gone."

   -Nestor, from *The Iliad* of Homer, *The Funeral Games for Patroclus*

    The modern reader has come to believe that people in pre-modern times barely lived beyond thirty. This false assumption stems from the use of "life-expectancy at birth" statistics to illustrate the relative quality of life enjoyed by people living in different times and places. If one attempts to measure the quality of life enjoyed by ancient peoples using this measure, things look bleak indeed. At birth, the typical inhabitant of a farm-based society before the advent of vaccines and antibiotics could expect to live to be about 35 years old. This is roughly half the life expectancy of a child born in a post-industrial society, such as 21st Century America.

    The problem with relying on such statistics is that much of the deaths that societies experienced before the advent of modern medicine were among children five years old and younger. This fact was related to the Spartan practice of infanticide and infant-exposure. It is also why many primitive cultures did not name their children at birth. As heartbreaking as this reality must have been for ancient parents, this meant that—barring involvement in war—a person who survived past age five, had a good chance of making it into middle age [40-60 years]. In fact, the term middle-aged comes from the medieval Norse. Someone must have been living to age 50; and if that was still just middle age, than some folks were also lingering into their 60s and 70s. Generally speaking, the young person who emerged from childhood intact, in ancient Greece, having weathered the mass of childhood afflictions without the aid of modern medicine, was a much tougher individual than his modern counterpart.

The Gods of Boxing

Once an ancient Greek reached the age of 12 he would begin practicing combat sports. By the time he was 16, perhaps younger, he would be competing. In late antiquity there were three age-based divisions: boys, youth and men, and up to five at some events. However, during the period covered by this book there were only two divisions: boys and men. There were no birth certificates. A man in this period would weigh about 140 pounds. Any boy that was as large as a man might be expected to fight with the men. Likewise, a small youth who appeared mature might be forced to fight with the men.

By the time a young man was regarded as physically mature enough to compete with men in athletics or serve in a main battle unit, he became part of the local military establishment. He would serve as a combat infantryman [if rich, as a horseman] or sailor, according to the needs of his community, until death, injury, illness, or the infirmity of old age prevented him from functioning as a warrior. It was common for men in their early sixties to fight in main battle units. In fact, there was a unit of heavy infantry men in the Macedonian army known as the Silver Shields, who had fought with King Phillip, his son Alexander, and after his death, hired themselves out to his successors. These veterans were all gray-beards who had been fighting for close to forty years, and were still among the most feared men on the battlefield during the wars of Alexander's successors.

Although men might commonly serve in combat for decades beyond their prime, this did not hold true for athletics. The art of killing on the battlefield owed a lot to technology, organization and unit cohesion. Athletics though, required high performance attributes from the individual. A fighter's career would typically span four to eight years, with only the very best fighting on beyond their mid-twenties. Those fighters who won contests as boys and men, or won multiple honors as men, were very exceptional.

While modern athletes tend to peak in their late twenties and early thirties, ancient athletes, as a class, peaked sooner, due to the medical limitations of the time. Many injuries, particularly to the joints, which are dealt with on a regular basis by modern diagnostic and surgical methods, would have constituted insurmountable obstacles to the ancient fighter, who had little more than first aid, diet, rest and massage to keep him going. Men such as Milo and Theogenes, who competed successfully into middle-age were extreme genetic freaks. Imagine not being able to have a torn rotator cuff or ACL repaired?

Even in modern boxing gyms age and the changes it brings on are a constant subject of concern for the trainer and the aging boxers they handle.

The Gods of Boxing

As one of my coaches so bluntly put it, "I used to be built like a Greek god. Now I'm built like a goddamn Greek!"

Despite the differences in ancient and modern medicine, it remains true that those athletes who competed at the top level into middle age, were, like Baltimore Orioles baseball great Cal Ripkin Junior, men blessed with a unique ability to survive stress and damage without sustaining debilitating injury, and/or to recover from an unusual degree from those injuries that did befall them. It may be for this unique ability to maintain and rebuild their bodies in service to their ambitions, that two of the greatest fighters of Classical Greece, Theogenes and Polydamas, were worshipped as deities of healing well into late antiquity, when such powers were assumed by the Christian Church.

In ancient times fighters such as Jersey Joe Walcott, George Foreman, and Randy Couture would have been revered far more than they have been in our time, for their accomplishments when past their prime. In a way, the ancient fighter was more mortal—in terms of athletic longevity—than his modern counterpart. It is little wonder than that he was so obsessed with his legacy.

Chapter 7
Fists of Honor: Archaic Boxing from Epeus to Tisander—1220 to 526 B.C.

"It is the sacrifice of human flesh. Yet it has its appeal."

-Donald K. Fried, *My Father's Fighter*

Pugmakhia was the ancient Hellenic* term for boxing. Pug means fist. Makhia means fighting. It was the most popular sport among the ancient Hellenes. Boxing continued to have great relevance as a metaphor for the moral struggles of the individual and warfare well into the late Roman period. As such, it retained a unique hold on the ancient imagination for well over a thousand years. The foundations for this unique appeal were laid during what historians would call the Geometric Period, circa 750-700 B.C. by the world's greatest poet and author, Homer. Believed to be blind [This point has been much debated.], Homer certainly understood the fighter's game from a sighted person's perspective. Whether his commentaries on boxing were the basis for, or simply the reflection of, his contemporaries' interest in boxing, is unknown. In any case, within one or two generations of Homer's composition of *The Iliad* and *The Odyssey*, boxing contests had become a regular feature of the Olympics.

The Archaic Period of Hellenic history is generally regarded as encompassing the entire 7th Century and the last 25 years of the 6th Century B.C. [700-575 B.C.] This study will expand the definition of the Archaic Period backward to include the Geometric and Dark Age periods and forward 55 years to encompass a portion of what scholars generally consider the Classical Period. Boxing, as a conservative art, appears to have evolved more slowly than other aspects of ancient life. But evolve it did. Wrestling appears to have changed even less during this period. MMA, on the other hand, seems to have evolved more rapidly.

Throughout this period every boxing archetype is present: the famed journeyman, Polydeukes; the old-timer, Nestor; the opponent, Klytomedes; the champion, Epeus; the challenger, Euryalus; the cornerman, Diomedes; the prospect, Laodamas; the trash-talker, Irus; the ringer, Odysseus; the legend, Doryklus; the pioneer, Onomastus; the phenom, Phylytas; the pretty-boy, Pythagoras; the white-collar boxer, Solon; the old-school fighter, Damagetus; the record-setter, Praxidamas; and the record-breaker and all-time-great, Tisander.

Imagine yourself stepping onto the Dug-up, re-raked to absorb the blood from previous fighters, and afford you and your opponent a level battle-ground. The afternoon sun of August beats down on your naked body. Your hands are expertly bound by your trainer, who squats on his haunches next to the dug-up whispering advice. The piper plays a tune on his double flute, and the rod-bearer of the sanctioning god begins to stalk you and your opponent with his wicked staff. If you run he's going to herd you toward your opponent. If you play for the clinch he's going to cane you. Your course is clear.

*Greek and Greece are Roman terms. The people that the Romans called Greeks referred to themselves as Hellenes, which was a term that identified them as the speakers of the language of Hellas, not as a particular ethnic group.

Figure 32.
Homeric Fist-Fighters

From a Geometric kantharos, circa 750 B.C.

These flat-footed fighters are broad-shouldered and possibly belted [as the narrow geometric waistlines might indicate]. Although a highly stylized piece of art, the combat depicted here seems to be functional, though primitive. The techniques depicted are most definitely less bio-mechanically advanced as those depicted in Minoan art some 1,000 years earlier. This, therefore, is not an evolution of boxing, but a rebirth.

Physiologically the representations of the fighters are actually quite astute. The triceps of the lead arms and the biceps of the rear arms depict the contraction of those muscles appropriate for each punch being thrown: the jab and uppercut. Though the fighters are differentiated by stature their technique is similar.

The bent knees and the withdrawn hips suggest a form of boxing reminiscent of the 18th and 19th Century British bare-knuckle tradition.

The Gods of Boxing

The stance and the possibility of belts suggest a form of boxing that has evolved from wrestling, perhaps as a hybrid. These two fighters behave as if they could be clinched and thrown.

The vertical fist alignments and the care taken by the leftward fighter to strike the taller opponent's face with the large knuckles—notice the depression of the wrist—suggest a bare-knuckle tradition. The appearance that the fighters might be wearing gloves on their rear hand may just be an artistic convention, or may indicate the use of hand-gear on only one hand.

The chambered position of the rear hand suggests an attention to power punching along with an incomplete understanding of punching mechanics. The rear hand of the larger fighter is pronated [palm down], and the smaller fighter's rear fist is supinated [palm up].

The fact that both fighters appear to be punching simultaneously indicates a dynamic art focused on a decisive outcome; athletic rather than artistic. A close look will reveal that the shorter fighter has his mouth open, either from exhaustion or exertion.

The fact that the taller fighter is depicted boxing as a southpaw with a right lead may simply be an attempt to show the chest and face of both fighters. According to Poliakoff [*Combat Sports in the Ancient World*] this was a standard artistic convention. However, the fact that the fighters seem to be stepping on or around each others' lead foot does suggest that this piece of art is a record of an actual combat in which a smaller fighter out-boxed a larger one, and, in so doing, forced the larger fighter to adopt a right-leading stance. The taller fighter has a narrower stance and his weight is shifted onto his rear leg, while the smaller more aggressive fighter has a wider more balanced stance.

The Gods of Boxing C. 750 B.C.

"But Lord [Apollo], I am defiled, since I killed him in hand-to-hand combat."

-Korax, at Delphi

The foundations of 8th Century B.C. Hellenic boxing were purely mythic; that is vested in the image of renowned ancestors who had, through the passage of time and the weight of tradition, become gods and heroes to the people of Homer's time. The only extant work of boxing art from this period has been presented on the previous page. Boxing was developing as a sport among the Hellenes at the same time they were developing heavy infantry tactics for close-in mass killing. Previously combat had featured skirmishing with missile weapons and dueling by prominent warriors. Boxing may have risen as a psychological preparation for the duel, and as dueling and skirmishing gave way to mass combat, may have continued to evolve as a tool for indoctrinating the ordinary fighting man into the ethos of close combat. Properly indoctrinating a fighting man to endure the psychological trauma of close-combat was tremendously important in the age of muscle-powered weaponry.*

The pantheon of gods worshipped by the Hellenes were in fact layers of conquering deities, whose worship had been imported by invaders, who in

The Gods of Boxing

turn adopted the gods of the defeated locals as subservient deities. Apollo was the eldest god associated with boxing. He was the god of excellence, music, archery, plagues, oxen [boxing straps and belts were made of ox-hide] and of boxing. Apollo was said to have defeated Ares [*War*] in boxing, as well as the manliest and most arrogant mortal of proto-antiquity, Phorbas [*Tribute-exactor*] who Apollo killed with his fists, becoming the patron-god of boxers.

These victories—particularly the one over Ares, who slept on a blanket of human skin—attributed to Apollo, hint at the ancient belief that skill trumps aggression in boxing.

The rudimentary nature of early Hellenic boxing, the importance of oxen to boxing, and the fact that the younger gods tended to be the patrons of the sport, indicates an Indo-European origin for boxing. It was not, as many boxing historians have proposed, a lineal evolution of Egyptian and Cretan boxing, but rather a practice brought in by the barbarian invaders from the hinterland.

The first of many boxers mentioned by Homer was Polydeukes [*Very-sweet*], the original sugar man. The Romans translated his name to Pullox. The second portion of his ancient Hellenic name survives in English as "dukes" a term commonly used to refer to fists up until the middle of the 20th Century. Polydeukes was the brother of Kastor, a duelist [and badass of the two]. Together they were known as the Dioskuri [*Heavenly-twins*]. They were, like Herakles, said to have been the bastard sons of Zeus, fathered on a woman of Sparta. Their sister was Helen of Troy. Homer referred to Polydeukes as a "hardy boxer", and by 800 B.C. he and his brother were being worshipped as gods throughout the Hellenic world.

There were a variety of ancient myths concerning the first Olympics. These probably reflected various starts and re-starts of the tradition, until it final caught on as an unbroken tradition. One of these early Olympiads was sponsored by Herakles, at which Polydeukes was said to have won the boxing, before Herakles and the Heavenly-twins accompanied Jason aboard the Argo on his quest for the Golden Fleece. The belief that Herakles, the prototype of the self-made all-power-fighter, acted as the first boxing promoter, may indicate nothing more than the antiquity of boxing as a method of training for warriors. [For more on Olympic origins see *All-Power-Fighting*.]

Later legends state that Paris, Prince of Troy, was the best of the Trojan boxers. Homer goes on to mention a proto-Olympic contest in which Nestor had won wrestling, running, javelin-throwing and had defeated Klytomedes [*Famed-Persian*] in boxing. Idomeneus [*Joy-abiding-chief*] of the island of

Crete was said to have been a noted boxer. Also, Odysseus [*Grieved-chief*], King of the island of Ithaka, a great all-around athlete, was touted as a superb boxer in the Odyssey. Although these are merely legends about great ancestors, the fact that these mythic boxers are often islanders does mesh nicely with the fact that most Olympic victors in boxing were islanders or from overseas colonies.

The one lone Olympic boxing champion that the ancients had credited with taking victory at one of the early Olympic false starts in the dark age that preceded the period when fighters erected victory statues with accompanying epitaphs, was Doryklus [*Spear-breaker?* or *–famed?*] of Tyrins, a dark-age stronghold, that would fade from history.

*Grossman, Davbe, Lt. Col. *On Killing: the Psychological Cost of Learning to Kill in War and Society*, Little Brown, NY, 1995
Throughout this superb study of human aggression Grossman repeatedly touches on the little discussed combat values of posturing and submission, and illuminates some of the enabling traditions—such as boxing—that have been utilized as psychological conditioning methods by military establishments

Epeus and Euryalus: composed c. 750 B.C.

"If, however, you do not perform your religious duty of fighting, then you will certainly incur sins for neglecting your duties and thus lose your reputation as a fighter."

-*The Bhagavad-gita*

At the funeral for Patroklus in Homer's Illiad the first event was the chariot race. After the awarding of prizes, Achilles, sponsor of the funeral contests, gave an honorary prize to Nestor, oldest of the war-chiefs. Nestor noted the loss of his boxing abilities due to old age, relived his most famous victories, and then thanked Achilles. Achilles made his way through the crowds of soldiers and marked off a boxing ring where he tethered a fine mule [a top-of-the-line pickup truck of its day] and placed a double-handled drinking cup [equal to a collectable German beer-mug]. Achilles [then the most feared war-chief alive] stood tall and challenged the men of the army,

The Gods of Boxing

"Lords of Akhaea—all you Akhaean warriors! We invite two men—our best—to compete for these. The man who Apollo helps outlast the other—clearly witnessed here by Akhaea's armies—he leads this beast of burden back to his tents, but the one he beats may have the two-eared cup."

Epeus [*The Noble*] immediately stood. He was large, powerful, and the most famous Akhaean boxer. Epeus grabbed the draft mule with one hand and shouted, "Step up and get that cup—whoever wants it! This mule is mine, I say. No one here will knock me out and take her—I am the greatest! So what if I'm not a first-rate warrior? [In fact, Epeus was a leader of support troops. It was said to be by his carpentry skills that the Trojan horse was fashioned.] How can a man be first in every contest? I warn you warriors—and I speak the truth—I'll crush you with body-punches, I'll crack your ribs to splinters! You keep your family mourners near to drag you away—once my fists have worn you to a pulp!"

After that menacing boast the army fell silent. Only one man summoned the courage to face Epeus. Euryalus [*Broad-enough*] was the son of King Mekisteus [*Noble?*] a famous boxing champion who once fought at the funeral of Oedipus at
Thebes, defeating all the Theban fighters. Euryalus was encouraged by Diomedes [*Heavenly-Persian*], who believed he could defeat Epeus and served as his second. The challenger was silent as he advanced to the ring and was readied for the contest. Both fighters were tightly fitted with a heavy leather belt that protected the kidneys and probably had a codpiece to protect the groin. Rawhide strips cut from a field ox [and thus tough] were wrapped around their hands—mostly across the knuckles to permit hard punching.

Both fighters squared off when ready and began boxing without a command from Achilles. They traded tight-fisted jabs briefly and then began throwing powerful combinations. The grinding of their clenched teeth marked their exertion as well as their efforts to avoid a broken jaw. The bout lasted long enough for both athletes to be covered in running sweat. Suddenly Euryalus dropped his guard in an attempt to pick a shot as he advanced, but Epeus had timed a crushing hook to the head—a knockout punch! Euryalus' knees buckled and he arched backward like a leaping fish—out cold.

Epeus picked up Euryalus and held him before his followers led him from the ring; his feet dragging and his head rolling to the side as he spit up clotted blood... He was still senseless after his handlers propped him up, so they retrieved the two-eared cup for him.

Analysis

Victory conditions are stated by Achilles and Epeus up front; the bout is won by knockout or exhaustion.

Prize-giving is more severe in boxing than all of the other contests. The value gap between the mule and the cup is far greater than any other first and second prize offered by Achilles.

Competition seems to be limited to war-chiefs. Even though Achilles and Epeus challenge all of the warriors it is assumed that the victor will lead the mule back to his tents—not tent. Epeus appears to be the chief engineer at the siege of Troy and Euryalus is obviously a prince with a significant following. Boxing is obviously the most dreaded event [more so than chariot racing and spear-fighting] and, as such, seems to be a test of moral courage, a prerequisite for military leadership in this culture of homicidal gang leaders.

The bout is not closely officiated in keeping with elite tests of honor throughout martial history.

The equipment specified points to an art form recently divorced from wrestling and dueling.

The techniques described differ little from modern boxing. Epeus is obviously bobbing and weaving and slipping punches like a modern pro, and Euryalus is utilizing a passive guard like a modern amateur.

The Gods of Boxing

**Figure 33.
The Belting of Euryalus**
Artist's conception

Prince Euryalus has his belt checked from the front by his cornerman Diomedes as one of his entourage adjusts the ties at the back of the thick ox-hide belt. Akhaean boxers were apparently heavy body-punchers so they wore a belt similar to that worn by the wrestlers, but probably with a cup similar to that worn in battle by spearmen.

The Gods of Boxing

The Prince, the Adventurer and the Bum

"Because your arms are too short to box with God."
  -Kid Rock, *Cocky*

The Odyssey [*Grieved-nobleman's-story*] is the story of the homeward journey of Odysseus [*Grieved-nobleman*] after the siege of Troy. Odysseus, the wily tactician and all-round fighter, had conceived of the Trojan horse, and Epeus, champion boxer and master carpenter, had constructed the novel siege engine.

One of Odysseus' many adventures resulted in him being invited as an honored guest by Alkinous, King of the Phaeakians, a refined island-dwelling people. At a contest held in honor of their guest King Alkinous announced the events in the following sequence: boxing, jumping, running, and wrestling. The king's son Laodamas [*Man-subduing*] won the boxing. He was described as stout, and a master of "dancing" which was done with another young man within a circle of youths who beat the time loudly. The dance consisted of tossing the ball up as the other leapt to catch it as well as passing the ball back-and-forth. After the contests and before the dancing Laodamas asked the aged Odysseus to show off his skills...

"...a man can lay no claim to greater fame as long as he lives—than strength and speed that he demonstrates with his own hands and feet."

After declining from weariness, Odysseus is taunted by the big fool who had won the wrestling and decides to throw the discus, far outdistancing the others. He then threatens to thrash anyone but Laodamas in boxing and wrestling and the king intercedes, declaring his people to be better dancers than fighters.

Having returned to his home island of Ithaka, Odysseus discovered that "suitors" for his wife's hand in marriage had crowded his house and were vying for his kingdom through forcing a marriage on his supposed widow as he had long been thought dead—twenty years having elapsed since his leaving for Troy.

Disguising himself as a beggar, Odysseus approached the gate of his house. As he passed the gate and made his way across the porch to the doorway to the hall, Irus [*Errand-runner*], a parasite who begged the suitors for his food and shelter, began to threaten the older smaller Odysseus with his fists. Odysseus, pointed out that they could share the shelter of the king's doorway and that he would—despite his age—bloody Irus' lips and chest in a fist fight. Irus responded that he would knock the older man's teeth across the ground with both his fists. Taking note of this budding entertainment possibility a large suitor named Antinous proposed a boxing match. His son announced that only the victor would have begging rights and that he would have first choice of the goat-bellies filled with blood and fat that were being cooked on the fire.

Before the match Odysseus asked, that due to his old age, he not be subjected to foul blows delivered by Irus' supporters. The suitors swore to stay out of the fray, and his son Telemachus [*Complete-fighter*] vowed to keep any oath-breakers at bay. When Odysseus gathered his rags about his waist the suitors were impressed with his physique—his 'bulging" thighs in particular—and Irus lost heart. Irus would have backed out but servants belted him up and pushed him out to fight, and Antinous [a primal Don King] threatened to send him off to a sadistic king who fed beggars to his hounds. When they put up their hands, Odysseus decided just to hit Irus hard enough to knock him down rather than kill him, so as not to draw suspicion.

Irus led with a jab at Odysseus' right shoulder, indicating that Odysseus was a southpaw. Odysseus followed the lazy jab with a straight left to Irus' neck just below the left ear, breaking his bones [either the base of the skull, a neck vertebrae or his jaw] and causing blood to gush from his mouth as he went down in a teeth-gnashing spasm, kicking his feet where he laid. Odysseus graciously dragged Irus back across the porch to the outer wall and returned his staff before heading back across the threshold into the hall.

Socially and technically the bare-knuckle bout between Odysseus and Irus has many parallels with the bare knuckle bouts of 18th century England, although the venue and dinner evokes medieval Scotland. The patronage of drunks, the constant threat of foul play, stripping to the waist, and achieving a knockout through a counterpunch to a vital target [the base of the jaw and ear was one of the 5 knockout targets favored by English boxers] as well as the bloody teeth-scattering nature of fist-fighting as described by Odysseus and Irus, all clearly evoke the atmosphere of the London Prize Ring circa. 1800.

Figure 34.
Odysseus and Irus Before the Suitors
Artist's conception

    Odysseus scores a straight left by stepping forward to the outside of Irus' left [lead] foot and pushing off with his own left [rear] foot.

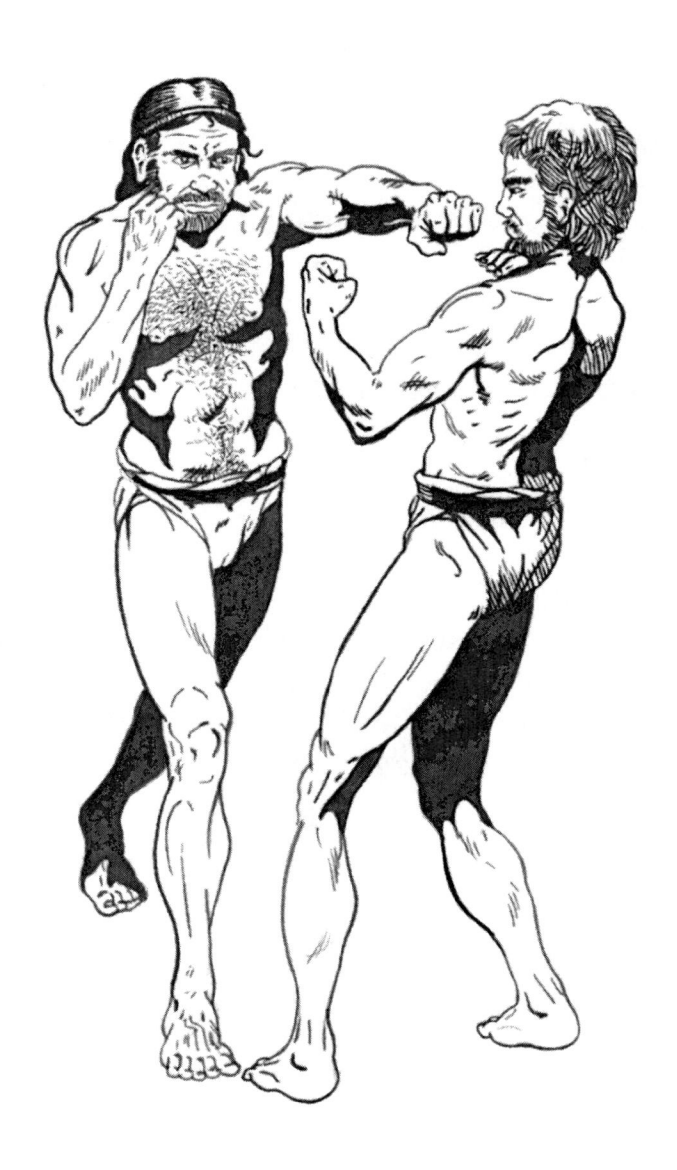

The Gods of Boxing

Boxing in 7th Century B.C. Hellas

"At Delos the long-haired Ionians gather together with their wives and children and delight the god with boxing and dance and song."

-*Hymn to Apollo*, anonymous

The Ionions were driven from mainland Greece by the Dorians, they sailed west into the Ionion sea, then south, around Greece, and east into the Agean sea, where they settled the islands of the Agean and the western coasts of Asia Minor [Anatolia or modern Turkey] which came to be known as Ionia. A disproportionate number of Olympic boxing champions were Ionian islanders. Whether this had to do with their seafaring lifestyle, a Cretan legacy, or simply the fact that they were skinny compared to mainlanders and didn't stand a chance in wrestling, can only be conjectured. Whatever the reason, Ionions looked to Apollo and excelled at his cherished sport. Likewise the colonists of Southern Italy and Sicily [Magna Greacia] were noted for boxing as well as other sports.

In 688 B.C., at the 23rd Olympiad, Onomastus [*Famed-scourge*] of Smyrna became the first Greek colonial to win an Olympic crown. This marked the first known boxing contest for at least 100 years, and Onomastus is said to have reintroduced boxing under new rules. These rules were probably based on the fact that Olympic events were now contested naked since Orsippus of Megara won the foot race in 720 B.C. at the 15th Olympiad without his loin cloth.* Without the homeric boxing/wrestling belt, Onomastus' heavier opponents may have had a difficult time clinching and holding and hitting, which are likely to have been common practices up until this point. Athletic traditions develop in such a way as to honor great achievements by imitation, therefore it is unlikely that Onomastus introduced new rules for boxing, but rather that he showed a new and more crowd-pleasing method of winning a fist-fight, with the result that judges set rules that would reward boxers for fighting in the manner of Onomastus—who quite literally seems to have whipped his opponents into submission. From the name *Famed-scourge* we might deduce that Onomastus regularly made good on Odysseus' promise to bleed the opposition. If certain 20th century gloved boxers specialized in slicing open their opponent's faces with gloves that utilized a particular stitching pattern** than certainly a warrior familiar with the spear and shield might learn to turn his punches so that the ends of his leather hand straps would cut like a whip.

The Gods of Boxing

Note: The chariot races were reintroduced 8 years later.

In 672 B.C., at the 27th Olympiad, Daippos [*Earth-horse*] of Kroton won the boxing crown. We know nothing else about Daippos except that he—like all Hellenes—was proud of his city which had been founded in 703 B.C. These athletes lived in a world where every city was a nation, and every able-bodied male citizen was a soldier.

Note: In 648 B.C. pankration was introduced into the Olympik program, and seems to have eclipsed boxing in popularity until the 6th century. The horse race was also introduced for the 33rd Olympiad.

In 616 B.C. the first boxing contest for boys was introduced at the 41st Olympiad. The victor was Phylytas [?] of Sybaris, an Italian colony known for its wealthy excesses and its rivalry with other Greek cities, particularly the colony of Kroton. "Sybarite" came to be used as a derogatory term. So Hellas was probably not overjoyed with young Phylytas' victory. The name Phylytas may be a derivative of the term for guard or guarding.

Note: This was the year in which the Etruscan kingdom established rule over Rome. The Etruscans would soon be importing and modifying Greek athletics to meet their own extravagant tastes.

The year 608 B.C. is the probable date when Solon [?] of Athens was victorious in the men's boxing at the 43rd Olympiad. Solon would go on to be the most influential politician of the next century. This year was also a year of sorrow for the Athenian athletes, as the Olympik pankratiast and Athenian general Phrynon, died in battle. Perhaps Solon's victory was something of a consolation for the Athenian delegation.

*According to Dionysius of Halicarnassus, writing in 25 B.C. [Our source for Orsippus was Pausanius writing c. A.D. 180.] the eldest Roman historian, Quintus Fabius, possibly writing c.500 B.C., claimed that Akanthus of Sparta was the first to run naked at Olympia—however, the Romans were very pro-Spartan...

** The authors' boxing coach, Mr. Frank Gilbert, of the *Loch Raven Boxing Team*, related a fight to the author that he witnessed at the *Blue Horizon* in Philadelphia during which one of his fighters was terribly cut up by his opponent who knew how to slice with the stitching of the Mexican-made gloves provided for that fight.

The Gods of Boxing

Figure 35.
The Triumph of Onomastus [Famed-scourge]
23rd Olympiad, Olympia, 688 B.C.
Artist's conception

Onamastus is depicted executing a variation on the type of "sprawl and brawl" tactics utilized by those modern MMA fighters who specialize in boxing. His opponents may well have preferred holding and hitting out of a clinch. His stronger opponent has unsuccessfully attempted to under hook his arms to set him up for punches to the kidneys or neck. Onomastus has sprawled slightly to his right by pushing off his opponent's left lead shoulder with his own left hand. He is countering with a circular straight right to the brow, calculated to cut and blind with his leather-strapped knuckles. This kind of short chopping right from the shoulder is delivered with a vertical fist. Such blows are generally frowned upon by coaches of modern gloved boxing. However, this is a punch preferred by bare-knucklers. Notable modern fighters who have employed this adaptation of the straight right include Jameel McCline, Randy Coutre and Tony Cygon.

The Gods of Boxing

Boxing in Early 6th Century B.C. Hellas

"Give a pledge and suffer for it."

-Khilon of Sparta

At the dawn of this most formative century in of the Greek experience—that is according to the ancient Greeks themselves—boxing was a martial art form practiced primarily for its value as a tool for conditioning young inductees into military youth clubs, essentially home-guard forces similar in function to our modern National Guard & Coast Guard. Combat sports, had, as of yet, not taken off as a cultural craze or professional activity. By the mid-point of the century things would be different. At mid-century, boxing would emerge full-blown as the premier national sport. However, this was due largely to the character of the boxers that were boxing at mid-century. As you are about to see, the first 50 years of 6th century Greece saw no steadily developing appreciation for boxing on a spectacular scale. However, for some reason the public did develop a thirst for boxing, reflected in a flood of boxing art by century's end.

"Wayfarer, if you recall a certain Pythagoras,
 Long-haired far sung boxer of Samos,
 Here am I. Go ask an Elean about my deed,
 Then nothing he says will you believe."
  -Theaitetos

In 588 B.C. Pythagoras [?] of Samos, an Ionian, was barred from competing in the boy's division having been judged too old. Determining the age class for a fighter was a subjective process entirely in the hands of the Eleans—the people of Elis who managed the Olympic agon. Apparently Pythagoras barely qualified as a man by size, was a colorful character who arrived wearing purple—the color of kings and judges—and was being dealt a raw deal. His epigram above is unusually boastful and hints that he defeated a field of larger more experienced boxers. We may assume that Pythagoras was between the age of 18 and 20 amongst a field in their prime. The Eleans may have judged according to new guidelines suggested by their embassy in 594 B.C. to the Egyptian King Psammerikhus who had been consulted as an expert on the conduct of sacred contests. Pythagoras may have fought as a youth had he lived in classical or imperial times.*

586 B.C. the Isthmian agon was instituted at Korinth on a 2 year cycle.

582 B.C. the Pythian agon was reorganized at Delphi on the Olympic model.

573 B.C. the Nemean agon was instituted on a 2 year cycle.

566 B.C. the PanAthenean agon was held at Athens, and would continue according to a 4 year cycle. The proliferation of these agons eventually encouraged gifted boxers to tour like a modern golf pro. In the future, gifted fighters such as Pythagoras would not rest on the laurels of a single Olympik victory, but campaign for immortal glory at many agons.

"Praise to you Polydeukes, that noble victory was for Khilon's son with fists won..."

-Diogenes Laertius, *Lives of Eminent Philosophers*

At the 56th Olympiad, in 556 B.C. Damagetus [*Submission-unwilling*] became the last Spartan to win boxing. At the victory ceremony, Damagetus' father, Khilon, one of the renowned "Seven Sages" of archaic Hellas, died of a combination of joy, old-age, and probably the exceedingly hot venue. Khilon would not be the last philosopher to die of heat stroke at Olympia. Sometime after Damagetus' victory—either in 548 or 544—the Spartan ephors [bossy old-people] forbade Spartans from competing in boxing or pankration because of the possibility of them having to submit, counter to their martial ethics. I suspect this ruling had something to do with the battle of 300 champions. See 548 B.C. below.

At an uncertain date the famous retired boxer Nikodorus [*Victory-giver*] of Mantinea drafts civic laws.

*In modern times amateur boxing meets are governed by a host of rules dealing with the overlapping of age categories, which are not themselves fixed, and are often blurred. As of 2004, *United States Amateur Boxing* recognized 8 age categories. Also, professional boxers in modern times have been notoriously difficult for biographers to age, such as: Charles "Sonny" Liston, George Foreman, and Marco Ruas...

Figure 36.
Boxers from the Korinthian Chest of Kypselus (restored)
Dedicated at the Temple of Zeus at Olympia, c. 580 B.C.

This boxing match is but one of the many scenes described by Pausanias when he viewed this ancient relic in the late 2nd century A.D. The chest commemorated the contests that accompanied the mythic funeral of King Pelias [a contemporary of Jason's Argonouts and the Akhaean besiegers of Troy]. The boxers were of course depicted nude, and boxing in the 6th century style. Since this scene is a reconstruction executed without a precise description the two salient points are the identity of the boxers and their musical accompaniment.

The boxers are Admetus [*Untamed*] and Mopsus [?] son of Ampyx [*Bothfists*]. Apparently the boxing contest at the funeral of Pelias is very similar to the bout between Epeus and Euryalus at the funeral of Patroklus—an undefeated fighter taking on the son of a noted champion. The outcome of the contest is not recorded but we may imagine Admetus extending his unbeaten streak at the expense of Mopsus. It should also be noted that Polydeukes—

patron saint of boxing—is said to have raced the chariot in the funeral contests for Pelias, and must therefore have either declined to box, or no-one rose to face him, resulting in an exhibition between Admetus and Mopsus.

Behind the boxers is a double-flute player providing rhythm for the fist-fight. Pausanias notes "in the way that flute-playing now accompanies the jump of the pentathlete", indicating that boxers of the 6th century B.C. fought to music, though the boxers of the 2nd century A.D. did not, and probably had not for some time. Though Homer mentions no musical accompaniment it may have been assumed in his day. The flute player providing background music for Admetus and Mopsus indicates a firm link between boxing and dueling [see Figure 27] and its aristocratic pretensions. The flute player would have been a slave or servant, as Greek citizens would not risk deforming their face by blowing or sucking. (One supposes that ancient Greeks would regard modern smokers with horror.)

Map 8.
Floor Plan of an Archaic Palaestra

This map is a deconstruction based on floor plans of later structures. One must keep in mind that a palaestra [wrestling-ground] at this early date was essentially the private manor and training hall of a combat-athlete-guru; making such a structure culturally similar to pioneering modern mixed-martial arts facilities such as Mark "The Hammer" Coleman's *Hammer House*, Mat Thornton's *Straight Blast Gym*, and Ken Shamrock's *Lions' Den*—a combination wrestling, boxing, fencing and dirty-fighting school for the martial education of the sons of the rich and the tutoring of less well-to-do [sons of farmers & artisans] youths with championship potential.

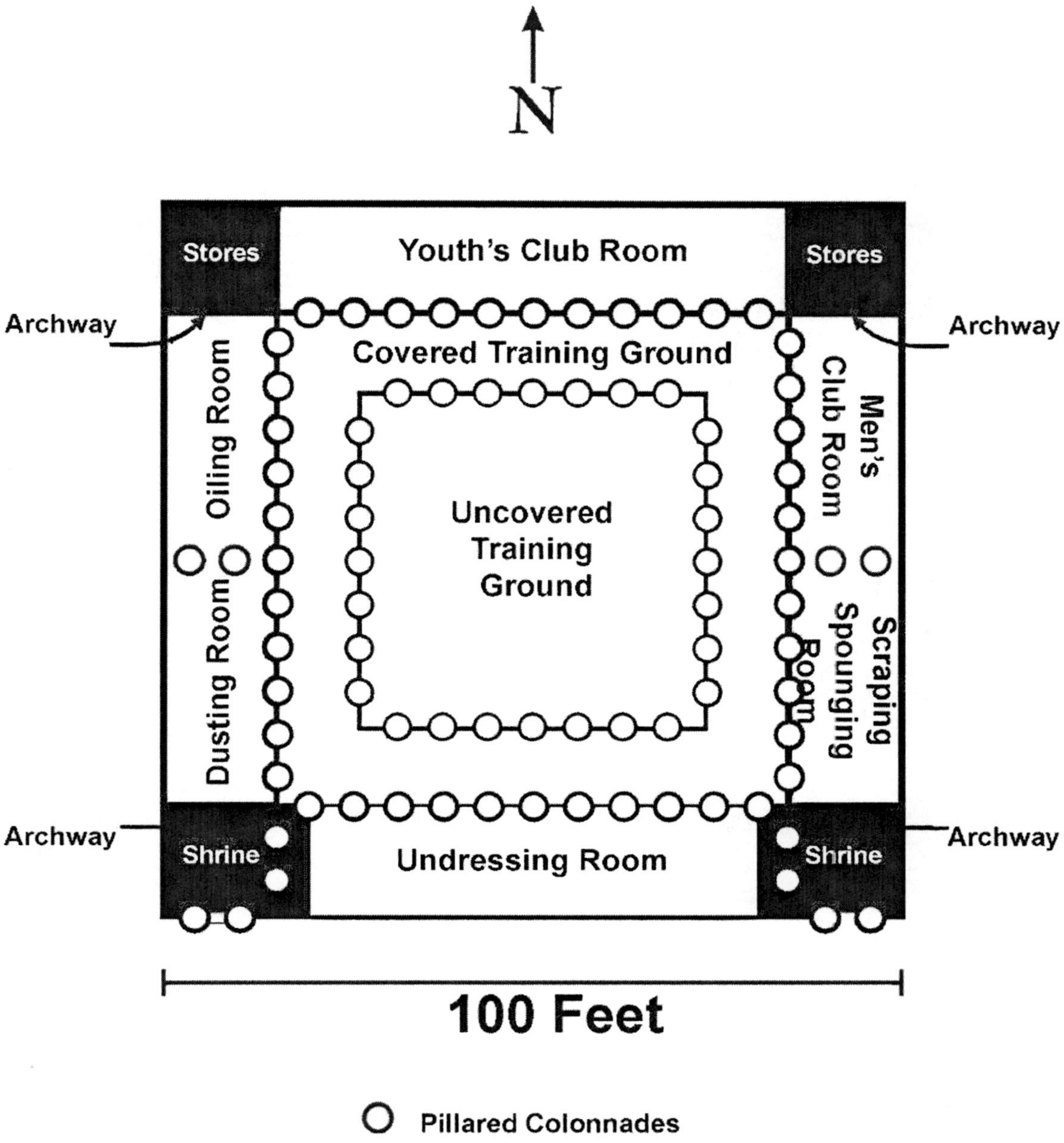
N
Stores
Youth's Club Room
Stores
Archway
Archway
Covered Training Ground
Oiling Room
Men's Club Room
Uncovered Training Ground
Dusting Room
Scraping Spounging Room
Archway
Archway
Shrine
Undressing Room
Shrine
100 Feet
Pillared Colonnades

Boxing in Mid 6th Century B.C. Hellas: 548-26 B.C.

"To live in triumph or in death to end."
-Theokles

548 B.C.: Praxidamas [*Active-subduer*] of Aegina, eldest grandson of Hegesimakhus [*Trainer-of-fighters*] wins boxing at the Isthmus [held in April]. There is no record of a boxing victor for the 58th Olympiad [held in August].

However, another sage, Thales of Miletus died of heat-stroke while watching the contests. Damagetus most likely died later in the year at the battle of champions between the armies of Argos and Sparta [probably in October]. 300 men from each force met in battle and only two Argives and one Spartan survived, apparently resulting in the hardening of Spartan martial ethics.

Boxing in the 3rd quarter of the 6th century is essentially the story of two men Praxidamas, and Tisander [*Greatest-of-men*] of Naxos. The records set by Praxidamas and Tisander remained among the most impressive boxing records for the subsequent 1,000 years of Greco-Roman boxing. Viewed in isolation, though, their records are yet more impressive, amounting to complete dominance in their own time. It is possible that figure 48 may well represent a bout involving Tisander, and, it is somewhat less possible –though it is an attractive supposition—that the elder boxer on the left is Praxidamas putting forth a losing effort against the younger Tisander at the 60th Olympiad in 540 B.C. It is, however, more likely to represent an older Tisander toughing it out against a younger comer in the 520s. Praxidamas was the first professional boxing champion, and Tisander remains the most successful boxer of all time, with four Olympik victories as well as four Pythiads to prove he was active.

"...Praxidamas. For he, as an Olympik victor, was the first to bring the olive crown...to Aegina, and by winning five crowns at Isthmus and three at Nemea, put an end to the obscurity of Sokleides [his father] and his family of toiling fighters..."

-Pindar, *Nemean Odes*

547 B.C. Praxidamas wins boxing at Nemea.
546 B.C. Praxidamas wins boxing at the Isthmus. Slaves are permitted to compete in the Panathenae.
545 B.C. Praxidamas wins boxing at Nemea.
544 B.C. Praxidamas wins boxing at the Isthmus, and later that year at the 59th Olympiad, and is the first athlete to have a statue raised—which was carved of cypress wood—in his honor in the Altis at Olympia, near the pillar of Oenamaus [perhaps the oldest relic in the Altis].
543 B.C. Praxidamas wins boxing at Nemea.
542 B.C. Praxidamas wins boxing at the Isthmus.
541 B.C. Praxidamas may have lost to Tisander at Nemea. Isthmian and Nemean records were incomplete during this period.

The Gods of Boxing

540 B.C. Praxidamas wins boxing at the Isthmus, and Tisander is victorious at the 60th Olympiad

538 B.C. Tisander wins boxing at the 11th Pythiad at Delphi.

536 B.C. Tisander wins boxing at the 61st Olympiad.

534 B.C. Tisander wins boxing at the 12th Pythiad.

532 B.C. Tisander wins boxing at the 62nd Olympiad.

530 B.C. The first treasury is built at Delphi, and Tisander wins boxing at the 13th Pythiad.

528 B.C. Tisander wins boxing at the 63rd Olympiad

526 B.C. Tisander wins boxing at the 14th Pythiad. Slaves are banned from competing at the PanAthenae.

"Of the city [Naxos] not even the ruins are to be seen, and that the name of Naxos has survived the ages must be attributed to Tisander, son of Kleokritus."

-Pausanias, *Description of Greece*

Tisander's record was believed by Pausanias to have been incompletely documented. Of the very best of the archaic boxers we know only that he swam out to sea daily from the port city of Naxos on Sicily to keep fit for fighting, just as Joe Frazier and Marco Ruas [the best conditioned fighters of their time] would do in the tamer waters of 20th century pools. Naxos outlived its most famous son by less than 100 years.

Figure 37.
Palm-Strike
Oinochoe Vase, c. 550 B.C.

    Both the fighters in this scene have their hands at eye-level. To the left is seated a judge or trainer who signals with his left hand and holds an open scroll in his right --possibly a boxing text. The onlooker to the right appears to be a patron or other interested but uninvolved spectator.
    The action is dominated by the larger, left-most fighter who is taking a long step in and attempting to post a palm jab to the nose; a possible knockout blow, but easy to defend against. His left hand is unwrapped, so we may assume an open hand lead to be his style. His right hand is wrapped to the wrist only and is hyper-pronated in preparation for a downward or lateral hammer-fist. Such a blow would fall between the left temple and kidney of the opponent, and would make ducking or bending under the palm strike a risky move. The high-held hyper-pronated fist could also be turned into a ripping uppercut—requiring a deft crouching slide step. However, an uppercut is unlikely since the wrist is not stabilized by the hand strap. This high rear-hand blow must have been delivered as the second element of a combination, and probably depended for success on exploiting the blinding effect of a missed palm jab or the ducking of the opponent.

The Gods of Boxing

    The right-most fighter has been driven back on his rear heel by the larger man, but appears to be managing a poised outward block with his lead forearm. He has bent his rear knee in an attempt to preserve his base, and, if he steps rightward with that rear foot, may be able to manage a plunging right hand to his opponent's heart or kidney. His right hand is bandaged to support the wrist for straight punching and uppercutting, while his lead hand is wrapped for knuckle protection only—which probably means jabbing to the head.

    It appears that the larger fighter is pressing a fairly gifted defensive boxer. If the orientation of the lead feet does not shift, and the hands of each fighter remain high, than the first man to step out to his right and attack the body should be able to dictate the next exchange or finish the fight with a heart or kidney punch.

Figure 38.
Italic Boxing Ring
Painted Italic clay vessel, Sala Consilina, Italy, c. 550 B.C.

This geometric piece from Italy gives some indication of what 8th century B.C. Greek boxing art may have looked like. The characters are heavily stylized and appear to be clothed. The fighters are clothed and are supervised by a rod-bearing official—with his back to the fence—who is endowed with a similar freakishly long right arm. The combat takes place within a fenced enclosure and spectators raise their fists in excitement off to the right.

The boxers' footwork is so fancifully distorted we may only note with certainty that their knees are bent in an athletic posture to facilitate dynamic mobility. The right-most fighter is being boxed against the fence as he jabs to his opponent's chest and scores with a straight right to the forehead. His more aggressive opponent is jabbing him in the eyes and firing a plunging right hand to the body, supported by a well-bent right knee helping to drive his weight forward. This appears to be the classic 1950s gloved right hand to the body. The referee appears to be using his long staff to keep the right-most fighter from backing into the fence.

Note: The elongated right arms may be a crude attempt to depict long straight punches going through their full range of motion.

Figure 39.
Parry & Counter
Rhodian Vase, c. 550 B.C.

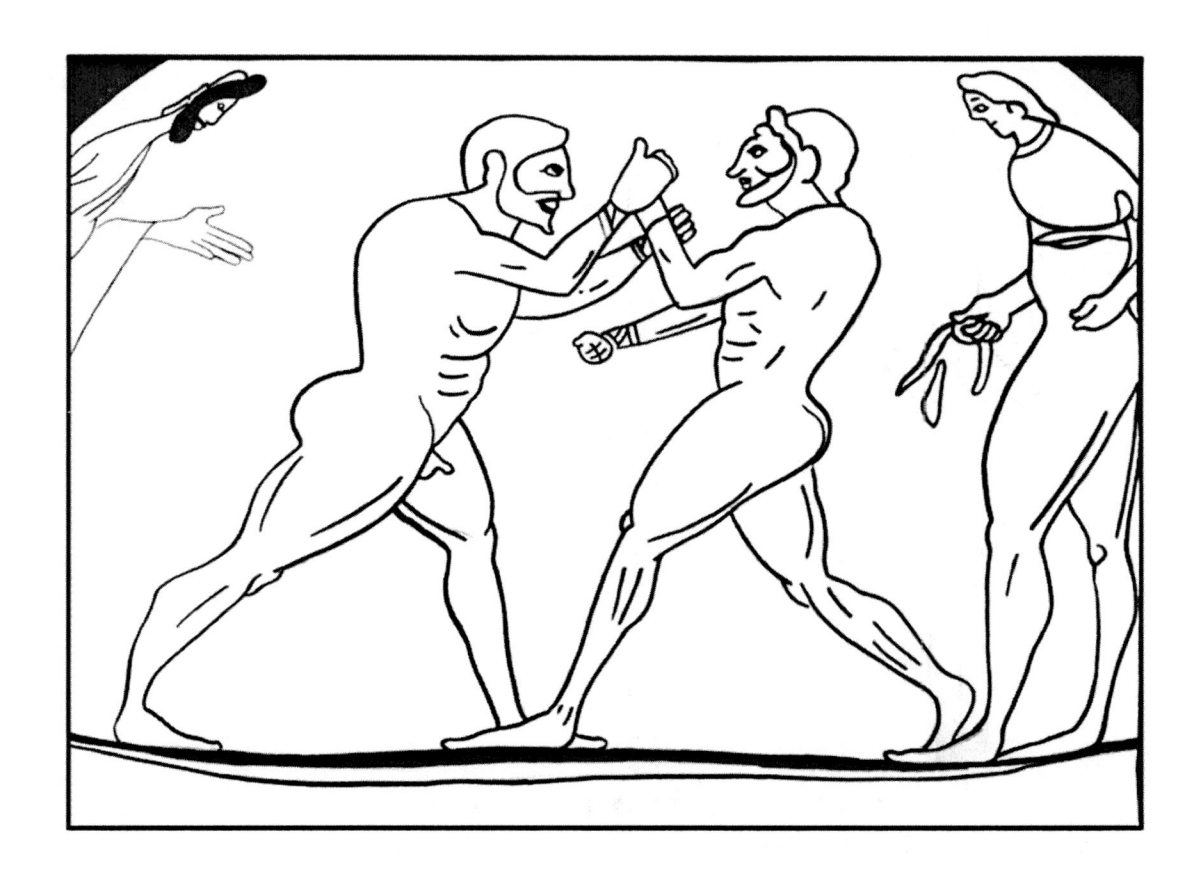

The fighters are observed by a judge on the left and a second on the right, both of whom appear to be taking a keen interest in the bout.

The leftmost fighter is halting his advance after missing with a left jab and having his straight right checked with his balance slightly forward. His guard is adequate for head protection, but his body is undefended.

The rightward fighter is either parrying or trapping [an aggressive check common in modern Chinese boxing] his opponent's power hand as he moves in aggressively with a straight right of his own apparently aimed at his opponent's solar plexus. His balance is perfect and the action of his right rear leg is optimal for the support of a straight right to the body.

Overall an excellent depiction of Hellenic boxing.

The Gods of Boxing

Figure 40.
Palm-strike to chin
Panathenaic amphora, c. 550 B.C.

    The usual attendants in the form of the rod-bearing judge on the left and the second with his bundle of hand-straps on the right are present for this bout. Both fighters have stepped in for the attack in an orthodox stance.
    The fighter to the left has taken a shorter step and has caught his opponent on the chin with a posted palm jab. His left appears to be unwrapped and his right is poised for a plunging straight punch to the body or a hammer-fist to any number of locations.
    The fighter to the right has stepped in too far and has eaten a nasty palm, which has ruined his balance and exposed his chin and throat. He is attempting to salvage the situation with a right uppercut which appears to be doomed to failure. He is guarding against a head shot with his elbow which has left his body terribly exposed.
    This scene has all the makings of a quick knockout.

Figure 41.
Thumb-boxing
Euboean amphora, c. 550 B. C.

These boxers from Euboea [Good-cattle-island] are fighting over a trophy tripod pictured in the background between the fighters. There does not appear to be any signs of supervision or assistance so it is definitely not a sacred event as there is a material prize and no judge.

The boxer on the left is the larger of the two and he jabs at his opponent's eyes with an extended thumb. The extended thumb seems to have been normal hand orientation for Euboean fighters of this period, and Euboeans were dreaded swordsmen. The big man is taking a long step forward, obviously hoping to follow up his blinding thumb jab with a hammer-fist. He bleeds from the nose, probably due to a slashing thumb jab delivered with the smaller man's left.

The smaller fighter on the right is in the process of retracting his lead hand and appears to be holding his ground. His rear right hand is held at a level too low for chambering a hammer-fist, so he probably intends to blind his opponent with a straight right thumb.

Overall this looks like the opening exchange of a long and exceedingly nasty fight.

The Gods of Boxing

Figure 42.
Finger Boxing
Fragment of dinos found at Tell Defenneh, c. 550 B.C.

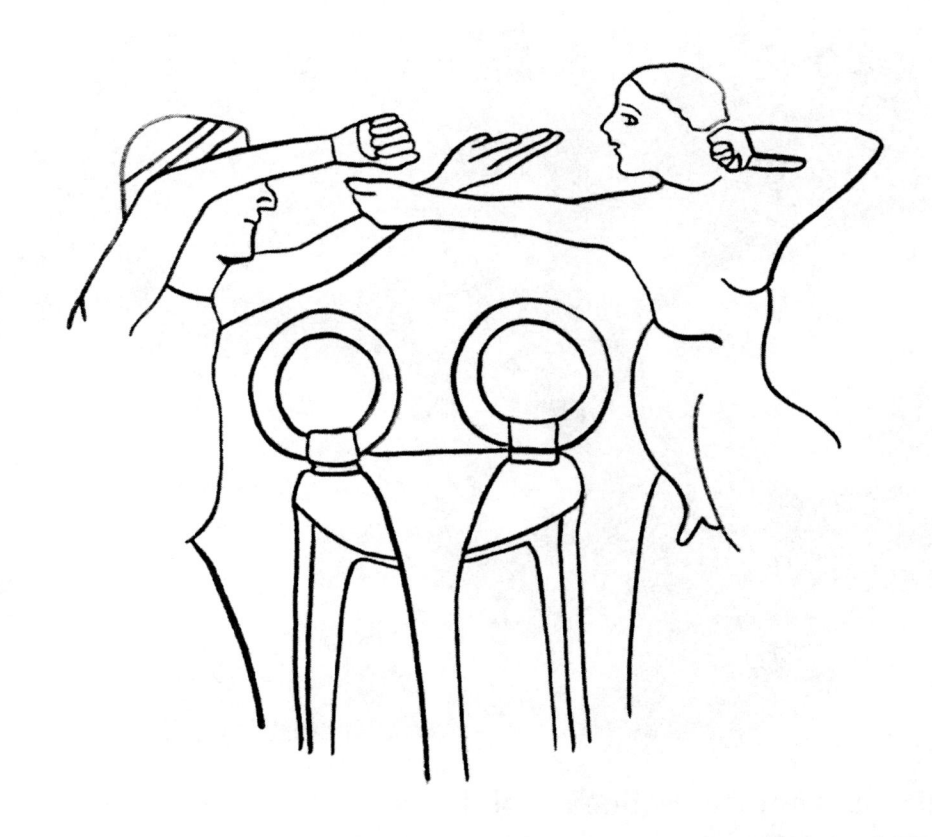

    In a fragment of the panel above the boxers is a defeated fighter. To the right is an official viewing some other event. Perhaps these fighters were being judged by a figure to the left who has not survived the damage to this artwork. The fighters are battling over a prize tripod which may have been filled with costly olive oil. Note that officials are usually depicted to the left of the combatants in archaic art work.
    The leftmost fighter is guarding his eyes from a thumb jab with a cross-arm guard familiar to fans of Archie Moore [1940s to 60s] or Ken Norton [1970s]. He is firing a finger jab of his own toward his opponent's eyes. This finger jab is executed in perfect form with the thumb riding close to the body of the hand.
    The rightmost fighter is a taller, younger left-hander who is coming right up the middle. He has chambered his left for a straight punch but is not in a position to land it, and he might be expected to fall victim to the finesse of his veteran opponent.

Figure 43.
Italian Boxers with Weights
Benvenuti situla from Este, c.540 B.C.

This seemingly odd piece is highly representative of Italian boxing artwork from 540 to 350 B.C. Five pieces identical to this one have been found throughout Italy, Illyria and Austria; and four similar though not identical pieces have also been recovered.

Like most of the cruder works of art depicting boxing of the archaic period these boxers are contesting for a material prize—in this case a trophy, without the supervision of a judge or seconds. These are more apt to represent funeral games given in a military contest [such as the bout between Epeus and Euryalus] rather than formalized sacred agons given at religious sanctuaries such as Olympia.

The dumbbells wielded by these boxers have been cause for much scholarly discussion. It may have been that these were simply training tools that the fighters raised in salute before going on to fight bare-handed. The dumbbell-shaped jumping weight of the pentathlon may well have been utilized as a training tool by boxers. The modern dumbbell was first developed by an English bare-knuckle boxer for physical conditioning. However, the absence of other hand equipment, and the tenacity of stick fighting as a sport in renaissance Italy, and reports of stick boxing among

18th century Northern Italians, leads the author to believe that these implements were wooden dumbbell-shaped clubs used for fighting, at a time when hammer-fisting was a common boxing technique. Subsequent pieces featuring dumbbells in 5th Century Italy support this interpretation as they demonstrate a finishing stroke, not simply a pre-fight salute. Let us not forget that Italy was the cradle of gladiatorial combat, besides which such a form of boxing would seem tame indeed.

    The dumbbell boxers fight out of an orthodox stance and make no attempt to guard with the rear hand. The stylized figures are not depicted in rigid poses, and there is a sense of rhythm in their attitude, suggesting the possibility of a rhythmic arm-swinging martial art heavily dependent on evasive footwork and guarding with the lead hand.

Figure 44.
The Nose-Bleed
Attic Amphora, by Nikosthenes, 530 B.C.

The Gods of Boxing

Both of these fighters are working out of the open guard typical of 6th Century boxing. The fighter on the left is bleeding from the nose—most likely as the result of a posted jab—and is intercepting his opponent's jab with the forearm of his own jabbing hand. His opponent on the right appears to be content to use superior attributes [reach, youth, speed...] to batter him in a symmetrical fashion.

Technical points to consider about both fighters are the neat and heavily wrapped fists and the high guard. Such heavily strapped hands would tend to be kept in a fist as leather hand-straps unravel easily when the hand is used for manipulations. The bleeding fighter is cross-stepping with his lead foot, which probably means that one of these guys is going to eat a big right hand soon.

Historians have postulated that the high guard [elbows held at shoulder level] indicated a lack of body punching. In light of the body-punching boast of Epeus and a mechanical analysis of Figure 39 the head hunting theory of Greek boxing for this period crumbles, as does the modern fantasy that "Boxing as practiced by the ancient Greeks involved minimal science. It consisted mainly of swinging- and looping-type blows..."*

The obvious reason for the extremely high guard of 6th Century boxers is the prevalence of thumb and finger jabs and the use of leather knuckle straps for cutting, which posed an acute danger to the eyes, which are the first organs that the human being will instinctively protect.

Black Belt magazine, November 2004, page 113, paragraph 2

Figure 45.
The Angry Nose Bleed
Attic Amphora, by Nikosthenes, 530 B.C.

This scene is from the same Attic amphora as Figure 44. The artist, Nikosthenes, painted four scenes on this piece. On the front belly of the vase is Figure 44; above are two wrestlers competing between two judges; on the back belly are two wrestlers; and on the back neck is this scene, which we have labeled Figure 45.

Both boxers are fighting out of an orthodox high guard. The fighter on the right is bleeding heavily from the nose and advancing on his antagonist, who appears to be awaiting the onslaught with a 21st Century guard—although any modern coach would be disgruntled over the wide spacing of the fighter's feet. This wide foot placement is the hallmark of young boxing arts in their formative stage—such as karate and Cretan boxing. Such a wide stance probably persisted among Greek boxers for so long because they were all schooled as stand-up wrestlers before undergoing boxing instruction. It was probably a trademark of successful touring fighters such as Tisander to use a narrower base; most of their opponents, however, would still be fighting like the converted wrestlers that they were.

The Gods of Boxing

Figure 46.
The Standard Combination
Greek vase, c. 530 B.C.

This is the most mechanically advanced version of the palm-jab used to set up a power punch with the rear hand as depicted in Figure 37, Figure 40 & Figure 48. Again the official and second have taken their usual places and, as usual, the figure on the left is pressing the action.

The fighter on the left is more athletic than his counterparts on the other vases and is attacking a competent defender, who is deflecting the palm strike by intercepting the supporting forearm with the forearm of his right hand as he readies a left uppercut. Somebody is going to eat it in this exchange! This is certainly the depiction of an action-packed fight.

Tactically the palm-jab is just as important as a blind jab [such as the long flicking jab of modern amateur boxers who are simply trying to interfere with the opponent's vision], as it is as a set-up technique useful for tilting the opponents chin and compromising his balance in much the same way that Muhammad Ali used the palm of his extended hand to keep shorter or stronger fighters off-balance and at arm's length.*

*Ali's antics and politics, and the fact that he fought tough, tough men obscured the fact that he had a tremendous straight right hand, and fouled opponents a lot.

Figure 47.
The Low Blow
Etruscan amphora, after 530 B.C.

The oddest thing about this scene is that the fighters are flanked by shield-bearers who have their heads downcast as if they were social inferiors—hinting at the high status of the fighters as well as the possibility that this was a military venue fought within a ring of shields. The Etruscans who held this competition were members of a society who shared little in the way of customs with the Greeks. Although they may have adopted Greek athletic practices whole in a technical sense, the context was possibly quite a bit different. Never-the-less, Greek, Etruscan or Roman fighters never complained about a low blow. It was all in a day's work.

The leftmost fighter has stepped to the outside to avoid his opponent's straight right hand and is digging in a vicious blow to the groin. His rear hand is held high in the archaic guard which chambers moderately well for straight blows and uppercuts and perfectly for angled hammer-fists.

The rightmost fighter holds his left high to ward off a lateral hammer-fist or deliver a hammer-fist or throw an uppercut of his own, but, by the looks of things, he is done. Without a foul-proof cup—not even briefs—he has little chance of lasting beyond this cruelly one-sided exchange.

Low blows of this ferocity were delivered by Michael Dokes, Evander Holyfield and Andrew Golata in the 1990s, and were effective even against a type of groin-protector that has been tested with a baseball bat! In the area of protective equipment the Cretans of 1600 B.C. were far more advanced than the Greeks were 1000 years later.

Figure 48.
Shifting Southpaws
Greek vase, after 530 B.C.

Flanked by two youthful seconds and two mature judges this appears to be an Olympian contest with the senior judge on the right.

The older fighter on the left is pressing the action with the familiar palm-jab, which the younger fighter has slipped. He appears to be a right-handed fighter who has just shifted into a left-handed stance in order to pass the younger man's guard who is fighting in a more relaxed and conservative fashion*. The veteran's only immediate option is to drill the fitter fighter with a straight right down the middle delivered in supination or dip for an uppercut.

The younger fighter's immediate offensive options include an elbow to the face, a short left cross, or hammer blows to the collar bone. Since he is being depicted pushing off with his left rear foot he is likely to choose the left cross before stepping out to his left and pivoting off the right foot to put his opponent totally out of position.

This scene appears to depict an older fighter reaching too furiously into his bag of tricks in an attempt to turn the tide against a younger man who is highly skilled in ring fundamentals.

*The veteran's shift of stance pre-figures Robert Fitzsimmon's "shift" that set up his solar plexus punch against the younger and larger James J. Corbett in the 14th round of their championship bout at Carson City Nevada, on March 17th 1897.

The Tools of the Archaic Boxer

"Take my cloak and I'll hit Bupalos [*Stuffed?-lot*] in the eye. For I have two right hands and I don't miss with my punches."
-Hipponax [*Horse-stone?*], c. 540 B.C.

Hipponax was apparently the Hemingway* of his day, and might be indicative of the kind of character that frequented the archaic mixed-martial arts school or palaestra [*wrestling-ground*] where boxers trained among massive wrestlers, amazing pankratiasts, and death-dealing monomakhaists. According to a famous trainer from the city of Skepsis, who penned a long lost training manual around 160 B.C., Hipponax was no slouch or mere trash-talker, and may even have competed at agons. The author claims that Hipponax was short and thin but also muscular and strong—and sounds very much like what modern boxing coaches would call a "head-case", lacking the discipline to ever be taken lightly, or conversely, to compete at a consistently high level. Hipponax's antagonist—if we permit ourselves some speculation based on the composition of his name—may have been a judge charged with casting lots from a helmet in order to match fighters at an agon.

The earliest Greek boxers appear to have used their environment to prepare for their contests. The palaestra was a wrestling ground with some supplementary facilities [the counterpart of the modern karate school with nothing but four walls a mat and mirrors], the primary purpose of which was to segregate the fighters from the population at large and to facilitate all-weather training by providing cover from the elements. The boxers used one another for skill development almost exclusively, as did the bare-knuckle fighters of the 18th and 19th centuries, and utilized their natural surroundings for conditioning.

The boxer paid his dues at the palaestra with donations of barley cakes which constituted the staple of the athletic diet at the time. Skills were learned and tested at the palaestra but conditioning was largely a matter of swimming and farm work, just as farm and lumber-camp work was a preferred part of the training of the gloved boxers of the early 20th Century. Informal ball-playing was probably a common activity at this time outside of the palaestra proper, possibly at the local gymnasium—an enclosed, shaded running ground where the five exercises of the pentathlon were practiced. The one hard-core conditioning method practiced within martial arts schools of the archaic area most likely consisted of picking, shoveling, and raking the wrestling ground.

The boxer's training kit would consist of the following:
 > a sack of barley cakes for himself and his trainer
 > a string for tying the foreskin over the head of the penis to prevent entry of dirt and the occasional unwelcome erection [which could be caused by pelvic floor cramps and pre-sparring jitters]
 > a flask of olive oil for anointing the body before training in order to protect the skin
 > a gardening tool such as a spade, pick or rake for softening and leveling the sparring area
 > jumping weights [dumbbells] probably used at the larger gymnasium or provided at the palaestra
 > a pair of leather hand straps
 > a set of leather ear guards for sparring identical to modern wrestling headgear **
 > a leather mouthpiece?***
 > a handball for ball exercises, supervised by a "Sphere-master"

> a scraper for removing the accumulation of oil, sweat, blood and dust after a workout
> a sponge for bathing

Dietary note: Aside from barley cakes, archaic boxers would eat porridge, fresh cheese, figs, meat as a relish, and watered-down wine.

*An early 20th century literary figure who challenged heavy-weight champion Jack Dempsey to a sparring session, and wrote some small pieces on prize-fighters.
**Probably not part of the usual kit at this date.
***Purely speculative on the author's part.

Figures 49-A to 49-E.
Reconstructing the Archaic Handwrap
From a photo-study of the Author's hand in November 2004

Figure 49-A.
A rolled 11 foot hand-strap; about the size of a can of snuff.

Figure 49-B.
Covering the knuckles from the starting position, with the loop across the palm.

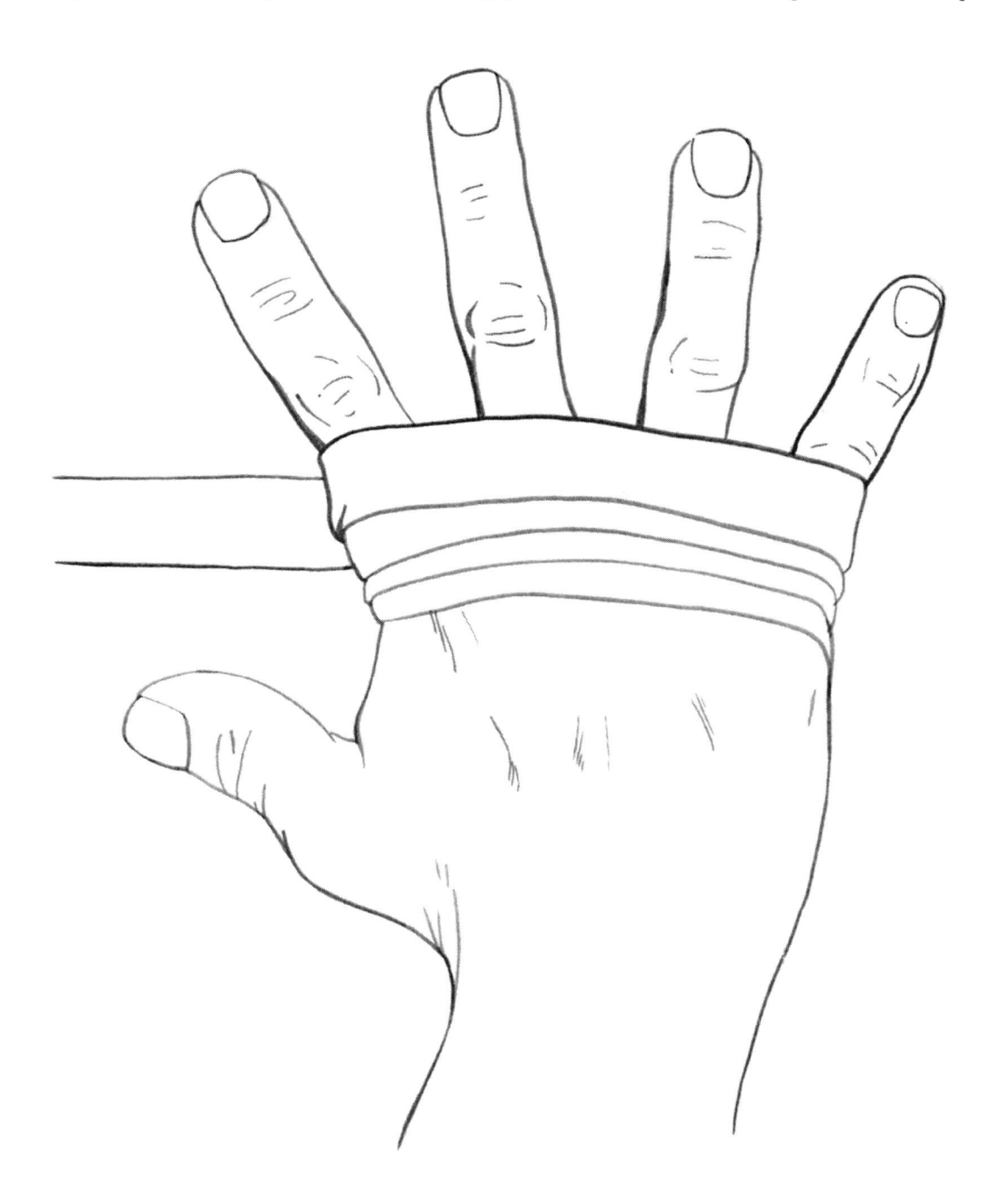

Figure 49-C.
Stabilizing the knuckle coverage by lacing the strap between the fingers.

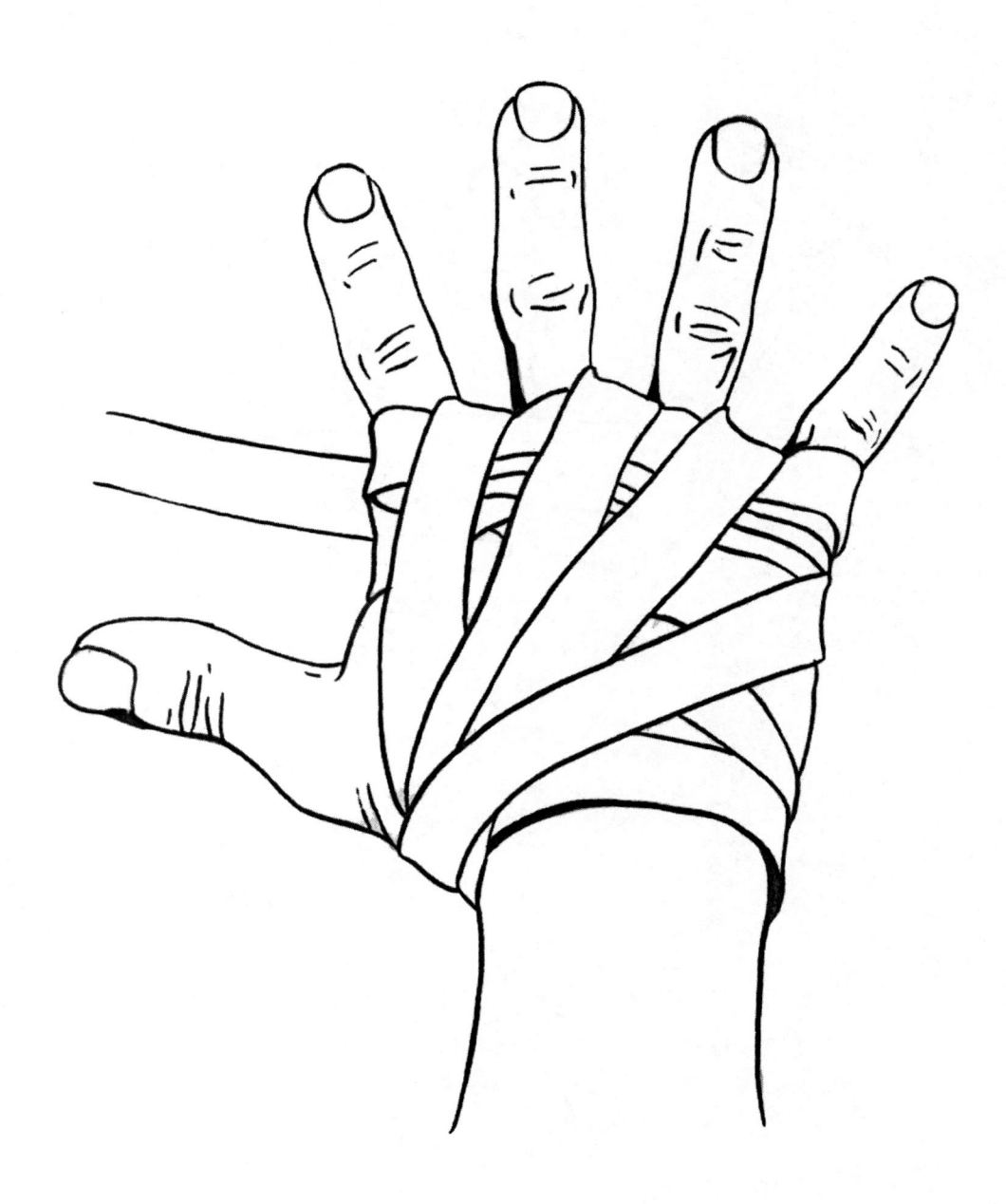

Figure 49-D.
Supporting the metacarpal bones [back of hand], and covering and supporting the wrist joint

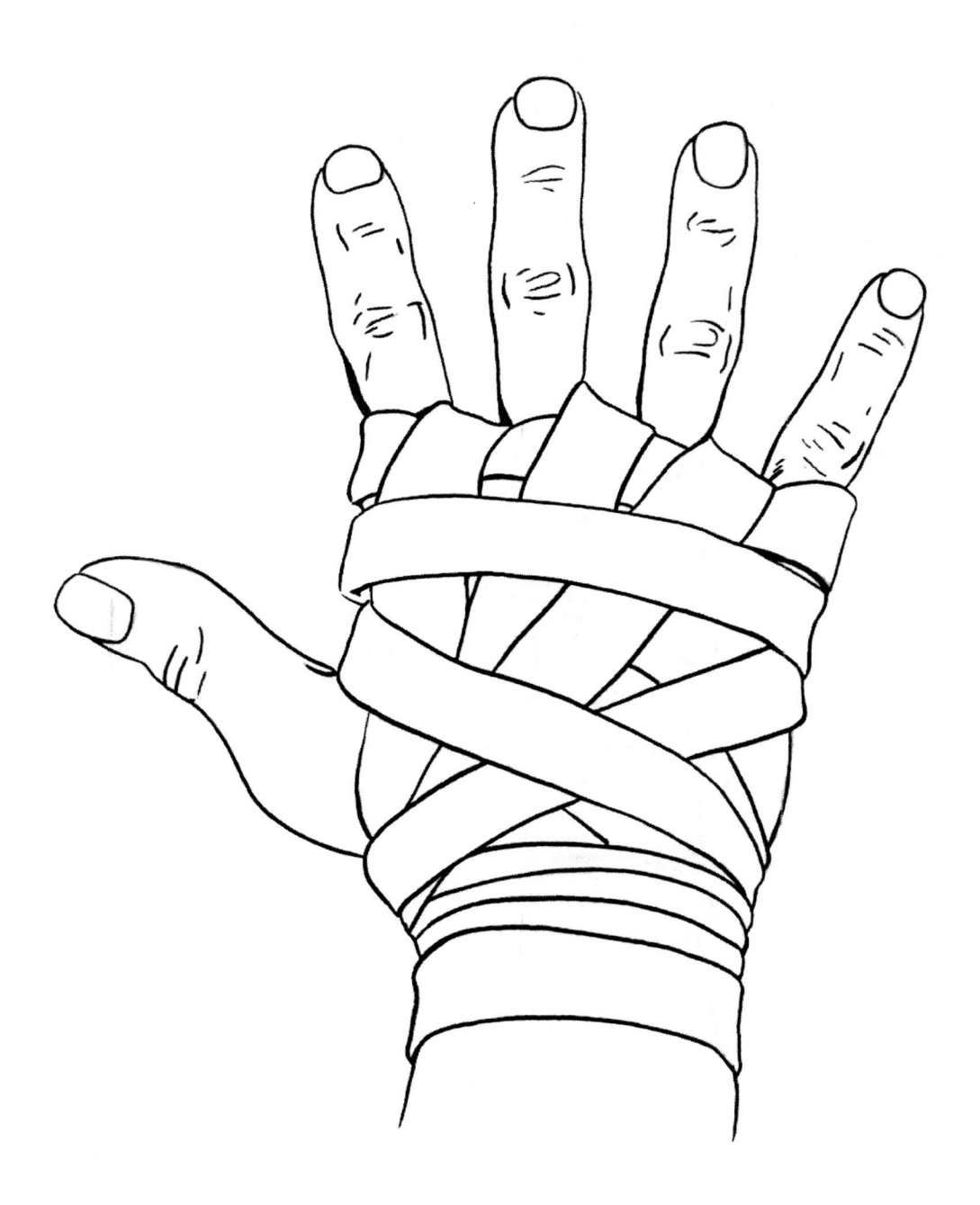

Figure 49-E.
The leather-strapped fist

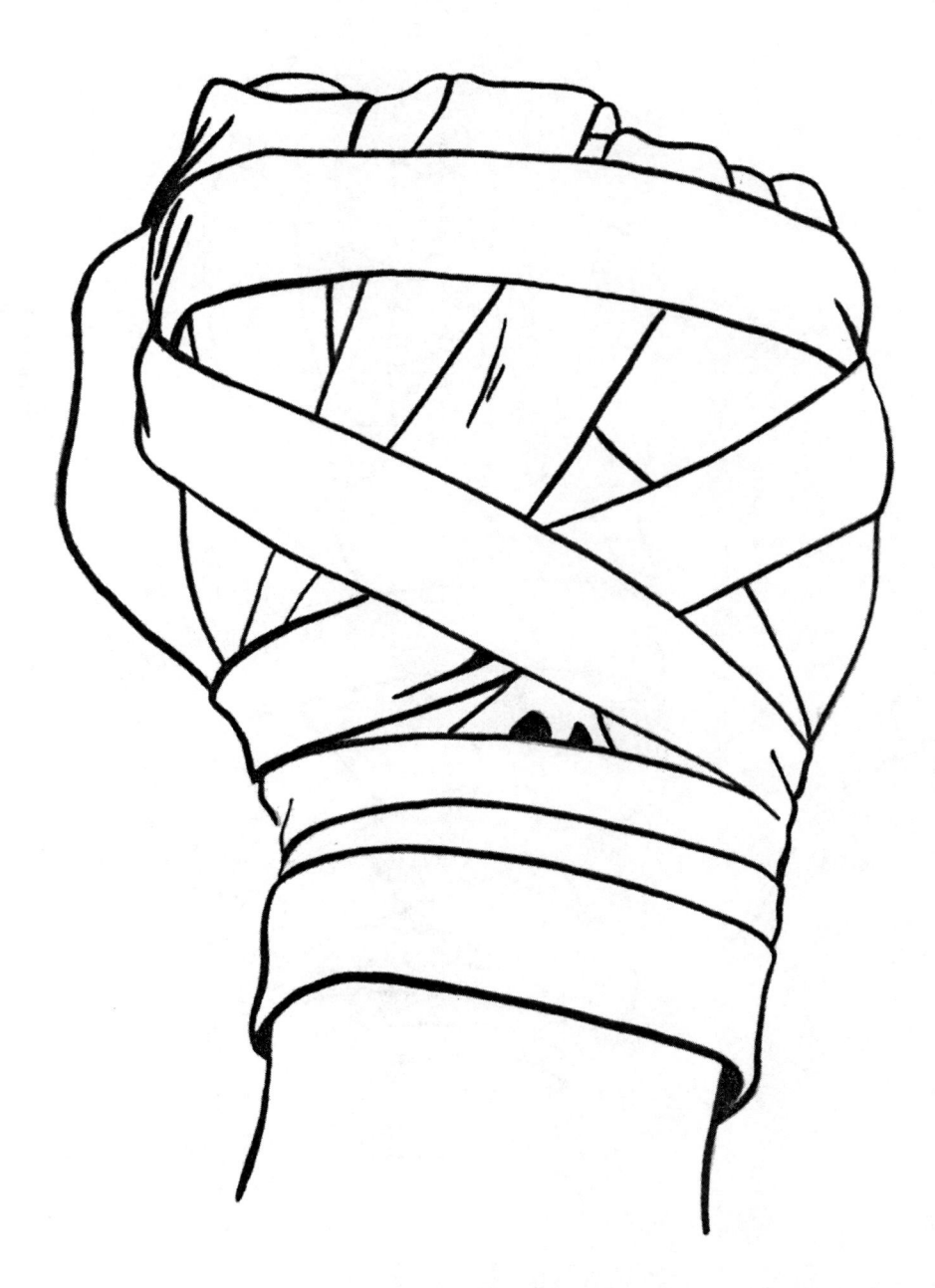

Note the tucked end behind the wrist. Wrapping with this leather is tougher than the old cotton-tie-down wraps I used in the 1970s. It only sets right about one in three times, and works a lot better if you use two straps: one for the fist to wrist; and one for the wrist alone.

The Gods of Boxing

An Analysis of Archaic Boxing Techniques in Literature & Art: 750-526 B.C.

"Boxing evolved from what people do for survival."
-Kareem Abdul Jbar

Strike Type of 48 Strikes

Fist	Digit	Palm	Dumbbell
62%	8%	10%	20%

Amplification of 48 Strikes

None [arm]	Linear [straight]	Rotational [hook]	Angular [uppercut]	Gravitational [hammer]
46%	40%	4%	6%	4%

Defenses Against 48 Strikes

Head/Body Movement	Active Hand*	Passive Hand	None
13%	31%	29%	27%

*Active hand defenses include parries, traps, catches and interceptions [hitting the hitting hand or arm]

A Stylistic Summary of Archaic Boxing

The conduct of archaic boxing was influenced primarily by the equipment of the fighters. The early era of belted Homeric boxing favored a more powerful stocky fighter, while the rise of nude Olympic boxing favored the lean fighter. These two archetypes [Ares and Apollo] will do battle in every fictional account of boxing until 450 A.D. Overall, the most influential aspect of this era is a raw-hide hand-strap that provides enough bone stabilization and cutting potential to encourage face and body blows, but not enough layering or padding to permit inaccurate head-hunting.

The boxing postures depicted in the artwork of this period have generally suffered from narrow or uneducated interpretations imposed by modern viewers. Boxing coaches usually can't get past the appearance of rigidity which is dictated by the constraints of the artistic medium and the range of the artist.

Asian-based martial artists tend to focus on hand orientations that relate to their own art and lose sight of the dominance of the fist and the importance of hand-wrapping to the ancient Greek art form. Academics, while offering educated perspectives on wrestling art, have always lacked an intimate enough understanding of boxing to offer reliable interpretations—E. Norman Gardiner being a notable exception.

In summation, the author must conclude that archaic Greek boxing centered on the "set-up" that is a blow or combination which the opponent was lured into in order to maximize power and minimize energy expenditure and hand injuries. Minimizing energy out-put and injury risk must have been paramount to a fighter competing in a single-elimination no-weight-class tournament under the afternoon sun of late August. The various open-hand blows depicted are conservative in nature and supplementary to the use of the fist. Clearly, the ancients from Homer to Hipponax admired the ability to punch effectively from the shoulder with both hands more than any other boxing skill.

From this base, the art of pugmakhia would continue to evolve. But the knockout blow with the fist would always remain its foundation.

The Cultural Context of Boxing in Archaic Hellas

Ancient Greek boxing was intimately linked with funerary rites, and psychological conditioning for the duel and mass combat. As such it was an inherently spiritual and metaphoric life-affirming pursuit that can make little sense to the modern, secular, zero-risk mentality grounded in a culture of complaisance and victimization. The modern mind might make sense of ancient boxing on technical grounds related to self-defense needs, or as an odd spectacle that places the ancient Greeks on a conveniently lower moral plane, but it is unlikely that more than a few anachronistic souls will ever come to understand the ancient art of Greek fist-fighting for what it was to those who practiced this most exacting of art forms.

Pugmakhia was a physical meditation on the virtues associated with living, struggling and dying, and, as such, it cast a spell on the human mind that has yet to be broken.

Chapter 8
The Air of Agony: A Boxer's View of the 99th Olympiad, 384 B.C.

War-singer felt like collapsing after every mandatory preparation demanded by the Fist Master and his trainers. And this last was the worst. They had just finished running the tip-toe circle in the dug-up at the center of the hand-struggling-ground. So he tried to stretch his calves with every step as he walked to the covered track on the perimeter to discuss the ever-narrowing field of opponents with his brother. The High Priest of Thunder-chief and the harsh Fist Master he had brought in from Dog-land, were intent on narrowing the field of fist-fighters down to 16 so that there would be no byes. No fighter would win the favor of Fortune by the chance to rest while others fought.

For his cunning brother the mandatories were an opportunity to measure the other prize-seekers while War-singer drilled. As he reached the shade of the covered track and took the water skin from his brother, a rolling thud hit the dug-up behind him, and his crafty little brother hissed, "Ooooh yes, that heavy-handed cock-sucker from Manly-island is eating the Descender's shit! That makes sixteen of you knuckleheads. They'll stop the winnowing now and let us get to our strategy and tactics. About time. We need to get you working the barely sack—I want you dropping eye-balls into the dust come prize-day! Fifteen big meat-sucking grunts, and I don't want one of them able to read your ode when it's done."

War-singer considered his mentor for a moment as he rinsed his mouth and swallowed slowly, "You know Fox-ear, you shouldn't be permitted to teach prize-seekers. You should be planning slaughters for some strategist against the barbarians. You remind me of the men that Father marched with down to the sea."

Fox-ear switched to his philosophical tone, "He wanted you for the Archer's art from the beginning—like a redemption—because of the pillaging fist-fighter from Grassland who killed our mothers back in The Empire."

"He never said such. Only asked me once if I wanted to fist-fight—never demanded a single punch."

The Gods of Boxing

"Look knuckle-head, Father and I talked lots while you pounded the piss out of the other boys in camp. It was so natural to you he took it as a sign. The Archer is in you; and everyone sees it except for you knuckle-head! After the way those greedy shit-heads fucked-up the contest four years ago for that horse-stealer from Grassland, everybody is on the lookout for a real fist-fighter. That's the second sign. That big bag of meat there that just passed out in your shadow, that's the third sign! You are the Archer!"

*****

The Fist Master led the column of fist-fighters, fathers, brothers and trainers through the reeking piles of ash and bone that rose smoking above the forest of statues in the sacred precinct to appease the gods above. The holy stench made one's stomach churn more than the anticipation of the agonies to come. The master halted before the angry statues of the Thunderer-of-Oaths that guarded the portal to the race course beyond, where the throng of Hellenes sweltered under the Archer's rays, anxiously awaiting the contest of fists.

The stern fatherly man, broad-shouldered, and without his front teeth, raised a heavy olive-wood rod and addressed the fighter's in a disconcertingly even tone, "Only six prize-seekers have earned the everlasting admonishment of Thunder-chief for dishonoring these contests held in worship to him. These images of the Thunder-of-Oaths were raised here with their fines. All six of these men were fist-fighters, and only the second, God-born of Woods-island, redeemed himself. A seventh will not be raised for a fist-fighter while I live! The murdering haunter that first defiled the agonies of the fist, and these four stupid boys from the gym, will not be accompanied by you.

Fathers, brothers, have your sons and brothers trained faithfully and done nothing criminal during the course of their training? Are they free from the taint of Murder?"

Fox-ear and the other trainers answered as one, "Our fighter is fit of body and pure of mind."

The Fist Master gave a long hard look at each fighter as he paced in front of the statues. When he spoke it sounded like he was gargling with gravel, "I'm no murderer, and would never kill a man with this rod. But, run, clinch, bite, kick or gouge, and I'll break your ankle. May the Archer be with you, and may the little-death pass you by."

*****

The Gods of Boxing

As Fox-ear strapped War-singer's hands for the final bout his sinister observations wandered like the finger of a strategist over a map, "Your right hand won't drop this one without breaking. You just about ruined it on that bone-headed goat-fucker from Oak-town. Circle right and pump your jab—finish flattening that nose. It's not completely broken down yet. Don't risk the finger-jab. Old kill-joy ankle-breaker here is liable to send your foot into the stables if he thinks you're gouging. Breathe dumb-ass, breathe!

His right eye is already puffed from his last bout. Twist the edge of this strap that I'm raising over the first knuckle into his eye. Cut him up! He won't see it coming—a stupid bastard to be a fist-fighter, and he doesn't have your wind either. People eat too much over here. Could you imagine stuffing yourself like that in camp? What a herd of fat pigs. You looked like the Archer out there against that meat-faced boy from Chambers, and this one's no better—just thicker."

War-singer found it easy to meditate while his brother rambled on in his cruel dehumanizing manner. He just breathed and sucked in his brother's insights while he rolled his head to loosen his neck, "You know the prize-scouts from Sickle-island have been arguing about you since you splashed The Master with the Chamber-boy's snot—that was beautiful! They want you for the tyrants. You could earn a lot of prizes and we'd be up to our elbows in pussy if we sail over there with an Olympic crown on your pretty head. The Strategist from Thought is here—right over there, with the Silent Men from Rope. There's another sign knuckle-head, He's here to see you win, probably remembers you from the camps. He was the Archer's pet—never lost a man of the Ten-thousand to plague. That's a fourth sign for your dumb ass. Now go feed this fucker some jabs!"

Fox-ear slapped him on the back as he stepped onto the dug-up to face the fighter from Thought. His jaw creaked oddly. But his mind was clear, his feet light, hands sure. As the piper sounded it occurred to him that he wasn't alone, and his opponent was…

Chapter 9
The Two Halves of Humanity: Slavery in Archaic and Classical Hellas

"The girl—I will not return the girl. Long before that,
old age will overtake her in my hall, in Argos
far from her fatherland, toiling back and fourth
at the weaving rack, forced to share my bed!"

-Agamemnon, from *The Rage of Achilles*

Life without forced servitude would have been unthinkable to the fighting men of Hellas. A life of servitude was the price one paid for surrender. The price of conquest was generally death for men and enslavement for their women and children. The ancients recognized slavery for what it was; the very foundation of civilized society. Compared to a free society, a society that tolerates slavery is inhumane. However, a society who takes slaves instead of committing genocide is acting in a relatively humane manner.

Subsistence level hunting and gathering societies typically exterminated defeated enemies—even women and children—in order to insure the use of the meager natural resources for which they had fought, only adopting enemy survivors into the tribe to replace their losses. Hence we should understand the first incidence of slavery as an act of mercy tied to practical economic considerations. In Hellas, prior to the 6th Century B.C. it appears that slaves were primarily family assets attached to individual households, indicated by the Homeric term for slave dmos, derived from the word for house domos or doma.

The particular type of slavery practiced in Homeric and Archaic times was founded on piracy and conquest: slaves themselves being the prizes acquired on raids and in battle. Ownership of slaves was the mark of a hero. There was not a racist component to slavery, and slaves were not viewed as subhuman, simply people without social status. A slave was unlucky enough to be at the mercy of a conqueror, but fortunate enough to be more valuable alive than dead. There might even be a chance for redemption and freedom.

The Gods of Boxing

Servile status was not yet a barrier to achievement. Slaves were even permitted to compete in the PanAthenaea in Athens from 546 to 526 B.C.

The institution of the dmos, intruded on every aspect of the fighting man's life. The piper who played the boxer's tune may well be a dmos. A heavy infantryman's 70 pounds of armor was often carried by a dmos while the army was on the march. This armor bearer might fight as a light-armed fighter, or serve as a medic, possibly dragging his wounded master off the battlefield, and perhaps earning his freedom. A boxer might even be arrested by a dmos for getting rowdy in Athens. The 300-man Athenian police force consisted of Skythian slaves.

For all of the slavery in Hellas, it was a place of relative freedom. This was an age of slave-economies. The sprawling Persian Empire was almost entirely populated by slaves. Only the Great King and his immediate family possessed rights amounting to anything like legally recognized ownership of their own persons.

Servitude in Classical Hellas

"Humanity is divided into two: the masters and the slaves."
    -Aristotle, *Politics*

Most of our information for slavery in this period comes from Athenian sources, and inferences from later historians chronicling the career of Alexander. War was the great provider of slaves in antiquity, and during the 5th Century Athens was constantly embroiled in wars great and small. In fact the Athenians committed at least three genocides during this period, which would involve slaughtering the men and selling the women and children.

The primary markets where slaves were bought and sold doubled as resort towns located on the Agean islands of Rhodes, Chios and Delos, as well as the greatest slave-market of antiquity at Ephesus, conveniently located on the Asian mainland, where virtually all people were slaves. Aristotle was convinced, wrongly, but only by a small degree, that the entire non-Hellenic world was populated by slaves and their masters. Hellas was also full of slaves and masters, but with a higher percentage of masters and, most importantly, a population of free non-slave-owning citizens.

The social landscape in Classical Hellas was peopled with a varied density of non-free-people. These people were not referred to as slaves. Slave was a term originating in the middle ages, when Slavic people were the standard servile commodity, bought by Norse, Byzantine, Arab and Turk alike. The Hellenic term had evolved from dmos [domestic servant] into doulos [laborer]. The institution of slavery in Hellas was now largely divorced from the idea of the extended household; and was being expressed in broader more exploitative economic terms.*

The numbers of slaves held by the two most powerful cities, Athens and Sparta, were astounding. The Spartans were outnumbered by their slaves by a ratio of 10 to 1, and for these slaves there was no hope for liberation or upward mobility. The Spartan system was similar to the 20th Century practice of South African Apartheid. However, in the bustling metropolis of Athens it was possible for slaves to own property and even earn their freedom, or have it granted in return for military service. At the peak of its power Athens was home to over 60,000 slaves, predominantly women, children and skilled craftsmen—including athletic trainers. Most able-bodied men were sent to the Laurium silver mines, which employed 10,000 male slaves who would be worked to death. It was these hellish silver mines that predicted the future of slavery in the ancient world. As the centuries of conquest and centralization took their toll on family-based institutions, the practice of plantation and even "industrial" slavery would become ever more dehumanizing, and eventually come to dominate the world of the prize-fighter.**

*Finley, M.I. *The World of Odysseus*, the Folio Society, London, 2002, page 47

**Thomas, Hugh. *The Slave Trade*, Simon & Schuster, NY 1997, pages 26, 27

Chapter 10
Ascension of the Prize-fighter: Deification and the Ancient Athlete

"…the inhabitants were freed from the ghost for all time. I heard another story about Euthymus, how that he reached extreme old age, and escaping again from death departed from among men in another way."
   -Pausanius: from the *Description of Greece*

People have often asked the question, "Why box?" In the Hellenic world the answer was easy, "To attain immortality." In fact, the process of deification in ancient Hellas can be clearly traced through a study of the afterlives of five famous and infamous boxers.

The first step is that of Heroization, by which the departed fighter is regarded as a malevolent ghost that must be appeased to avoid coming under his curse or to elicit a favor at the place of his epitaph. This is essentially a belief in haunting. This process results from the breaking of a taboo by the departed during his life. These taboos gain significance by the fact they were broken by a man who was questing heroically before the gods. In Hellas, hero, in no way, meant "good-guy". Heroes could be evil.

The taboos include: profane uses of the hand like striking the face, causing cranial bleeding and killing an opponent in sacral combat; as well as denying a hero's rites of appeasement; or challenging the status of kings* or gods through intentionally heroic acts. Boxers, by simply boxing at sacral venues like Olympia, are bound to break some of these taboos, and possibly all of them. What follows is a chronological overview of the circumstances surrounding the initial heroizing of five boxers. It is worth noting that only boxers and all-power-fighters came to be worshipped as heroes, and that all of these deified prize-fighters competed in the Classical period.

Glaukos [*Gray-fish*] of Karystos, was the son of a simple farmer who gained great renown as an example of arête, and also appears to have earned the ire of the Tyrant Gelon. Glaukos was a cautionary figure whose excellence did not save him from tragedy.

The Gods of Boxing

Kleomedes [*Lion-of-Persia*] of Astypalia came to be worshipped as a malevolent ghost after intentionally killing his opponent with a body blow, and then going insane and murdering school children after being levied with a huge fine.

Diognetes of Crete [*Heavenly-?*] was fined, exiled, and worshipped as a hero after the man he defeated for the Olympic crown died [possibly of heat-stroke] after the bout.

Theogenes [*God-born*] of Thasos, earned his infamous status as a maniacally competitive athlete who was irreverent and unbeatable. He atoned in later life as a philanthropist, but was even convicted of a crime after his death—a crime of murder committed by his status when it fell on a former opponent! It would take a tragic-comedy accident, a civil suit, a famine, a Delphic prophecy** and a lucky fishing expedition to build his supernatural status. He was the exemplar of over-reaching arrogance or hubris.

Euthymus [*Grace-speaker*] of Lokri, for whom Theogenes was fined for spiting, was revered for single-handedly abolishing a cult of human sacrifice through a heroic act on his way home from an Olympic contest. He was the exemplar of pure virtue.

Why was the boxer so likely to be damned and/or worshipped? There is the element of meditative purification, without which no prophet, from Moses to the Buda to Mohammad, would have amounted to anything on the religious stage. Prize-seeking was a sacral event for which a contestant must undergo a period of purification. The boxer and all-power-fighter were unique among the prize-seekers in being at risk for breaking such severe Indo-European taboos. The ambivalent, or even hostile, cult of the hero awaited for the purified prize-fighter who committed a taboo act before the gods. Persistent belief in the positive qualities of the heroized athlete could lead to a heightened reverence for his ghost, and the possibility of complete deification.

The second step in deification is the belief in divine conception. This would effectively raise the divine status of the departed athlete from ghost to something equivalent to a patron saint. Apollo, alone among ascendant prehistoric boxers, was believed to have been conceived by divine parents [Zeus and Leto]. Herakles and Polydeukes were divine/mortal bastards fathered by Zeus during his predatory sexual escapades among mortal women. Likewise, the historic boxers Glaukos, Theogenes and Euthymus were said to have been fathered by divine forces, but born to mortal women.

Glaukos was thought to be the son of a minor sea god by the same name. Theogenes was the son of Timosthenes [*Honorable-strength*], High Priest of Herakles. Legend had it that Herakles took possession of Timosthenes to

The Gods of Boxing

impregnate the priest's wife. Euthymus was said to be the son of the enchanted river Kaekinus [a god-river that was responsible for keeping the peace between rival species of grasshoppers]. These divinely favored individuals were usually associated with rivers [male deities], sea-spray or sacred trees such as the oak or olive. The ancient Hellenic appreciation for the natural world and the importance of revering departed ancestors was far closer to the belief systems of Native Americans than to the state-sponsored monotheistic religions [Christianity, Zoroasterism and Islam] that superseded the Hellenic mythos in late antiquity.

The final phase of deification is ascension. A belief in ascension comes into being at that point in time when awe for a divinely conceived hero becomes more widespread or intense. This heightened sense of awe is associated with good deeds attributed to the hero in life and/or ominous portents associated with his death or memorial. Hereafter the hero is believed to have been accepted by the gods as an immortal, and is expected to intercede in supernatural affairs, including healing, on behalf of his worshippers.

The two historic boxers to achieve ascension, Theogenes and Euthymus, actually fought each other in 480 B.C. This was the ancient world's version of Ali-Frazier in Manila. While Theogenes was victorious over Euthymus he was fined and banned from boxing at the Olympics, for he had to forfeit in the final round of the all-power-thing because he was gassed from his bout with Euthymus. The priests judged him guilty of hubris and spite against Euthymus. Euthymus had won the previous Olympiad and went on to win the next two. This leaves him tied for second place in Olympic boxing with Teofilo Stevenson of Cuba [A.D. 1972, 1976 & 1980].

Theogenes achieved ascension based on serious of incidents involving his Thasian statue and was worshipped until late antiquity [about a 700 year run] as a god of healing.

Euthymus won immortality by thwarting a brutal religious practice in the small town of Temesa. His ship was blow off course on his return from Olympia. Discovering that he had arrived just in time to see a unique sacrificial ceremony, he went to the temple of the local hero. This hero was said to be the ghost of a member of the crew of Odysseus. This sailor had gotten drunk and raped a local virgin, and had been stoned to death.

Some time before Euthymus' arrival there had been a killing spree in Temesa. The victims were mostly children and the elderly. The inhabitants, before abandoning their town, made a pilgrimage to the Delphic Oracle of Apollo. The Oracle forbade them to flee, and ordered them to propitiate the ghost of the hero by building him a temple and offering him for a wife, each year, the best-looking virgin woman of Temesa. After hearing about this Euthymus decided that he wanted to enter the temple and see the virgin.

Euthymus found the young woman to be quite attractive. She begged him to save her, saying that she would marry him if he did. Ethymus put on his armor and geared up for war. This alone is an indication of how dangerous travel for athletes was at the time. Imagine the World Heavyweight Champion packing a Kevlar vest, helmet, and assault rifle every time he flew to Vegas to defend his title!

Euthymus waited for the ghost to appear. The Ghost was named Lycas [*Wolf*]. Lycas was described by Pausanius, who examined a portrait of him as, "Horribly black in color, and exceedingly dreadful in all his appearance, he had a wolf's skin thrown round him as a garment."

Euthymus won the fight in the temple and seems to have pursued Lycas down to the shore and drowned him in the sea. A modern analogy would be an encounter in a cult compound between an abusive pastor and Vitali Klitchko. From a modern viewpoint this cult of Lycas just reeks of a serial killer and his accomplices setting themselves up to prey on the young women of the town. Perhaps the priests were selling sex slaves to the Korinthians or Etruscans. One suspects that the articulate and worldly Euthymus saw through this brutal scheme and saved the ignorant townspeople from this cult.

Euthymus and the girl were married at Temesa in a lavish wedding. He then abolished the cult, and traveled home with his wife to live to an extreme old age. He was honored by the famous poet Menander as the very exemplar of manly virtue. He was also said to have escaped death, having "departed from among men in another way."

Euthymus, [*Grace-speaker*] embodied the primal Indo-European traditions of the sacred river, the speaking of sacred words and the power of the taboo hand***. He escaped even the grim fate of becoming a tormented and put upon god. He alone, among the men, heroes, and gods of ancient Hellas was said to have escaped the sorrows of life, to become the last and most loved of heroes.

*In the year 212 B.C., Kleitomakhus [*Eternally-glorious-fighter*], who had achieved great fame by winning wrestling [without a fall], boxing, and all-power-fighting, all on the same day at Korinth, was targeted by the Ptolemaic King of Egypt [richest man in the world], who had the best young boxer in the world hired and trained specifically to defeat the aging Kleitomakhus at Olympia.

** Apollo, god of boxing, for whom the Delphic Oracle spoke, seems to have looked after his fellow boxers through favorable prophecies.
***Spence, Lewis. *Druids: Their Origins and History*, Barnes & Noble, NY pgs 14-15, 91-93, 170-171

Chapter 11
Fists of Fame: Classical Boxing from Glaukos to Satyrus, 524 to 325 B.C.

"The defect of this style was the stiff high guard with the left hand, which cramped the attack and encouraged the use of downward chopping blows."
 -E Norman Gardiner, c.1908

    The quote above is given as published in *Athletics in the Ancient World*, first released in 1930 [the year of Gardiner's death] but based on his 1910 book *Greek Athletic Sports and Festivals*. Therefore Gardiner completed his study of ancient Greek boxing no later than 1908. These dates are very important, as Gardiner's interpretation of Classical Greek boxing remains the academic standard into the 21st Century; and because the proper focus for the study of boxing in the Classical period is the study of technique, as virtually all of the extant source material for this period consists of technical studies of boxing methods, which must have constituted something of a craze since a massive body of tableware from this period was decorated with these images. Most of the scenes in this chapter are from Athenian tableware.
    The state of the art of boxing at the time Gardiner first wrote his thesis is of paramount importance for anyone wishing to deconstruct Gardiner's theory of Classical boxing in order to preserve those insights of his which remain useful, and debunk those myths which have grown out of the distorted image of ancient boxing as seen through the eyes of a 19th Century amateur English boxer. A deconstruction of Gardiner's thesis is preferred here because most of his deductions are sustainable, and also, because virtually everyone who has undertaken a serious study of ancient boxing in the intervening years have come to understand and accept ancient Greek boxing through his unique and flawed prism.
    Gardiner's Boxing Thesis suffers from the same ill that afflicts the majority of ancient athletic studies, which is the blurring of time periods as opposed to a chronological reconstruction; and analysis by analogy instead of through a biomechanical reading. The strength and truth of his thesis is the depiction of a mobile two-handed punching art which was based on

"scientific" lineal punching but relied upon some rather crude practices to force the issue, namely "downward chopping blows" [hammer-fists] and wildly reaching uppercuts [often mistaken for hooks] and some rather girlie looking long range trapping, stopping and parrying techniques. His observation that ancient Greek boxing was more a kin to early 20th Century American gloved boxing than to late 19th Century English boxing is right on target. But as an amateur level English boxer he lacked the tools to explore the ramifications of his astute observation.

A Revised Thesis for Classical Greek Boxing should state the following: The orthodox method of boxing for this period was founded on a left lead, a high guard and a belief in two-handed combination punching. Therefore, the basic principles of boxing were the same for the Classical Greek boxer c. 500 B.C. and the best boxers of the American Gloved era c.1950. Due to the lack of padded handgear among the Greeks and zero-tolerance for clinching in ancient contests, and rules against "rabbit" punching [hammer-fisting] among the 20th Century Americans, Classical Greek boxing differed from Classical American boxing on three primary points:

1. The Greeks were apt to shift leads in decisive exchanges in order to apply the hammer-fist to head and body, the kidney being a likely target.
2. The Greeks favored vertical punches that protected their exposed thumbs instead of the more powerful pronated punches of the modern American fighter.
3. The Greeks favored "High-handedness" [trapping] a controlling slap which is a common defense in Chinese Boxing, to the parry and palm catch, due to their severe clinch restrictions and light hand gear.

Technical Notes
We no longer see the eye-poking tactics of the archaic boxer. This was not due to a rules restriction, but probably to effective countermeasures, such as punching the fingers and thumb [Sparring trials by the author with gloves and goggles against a partner with headgear and taped finger-tips established this tactic as a superior countermeasure to the finger and thumb punch to the eye.] The high elbows of the Greek boxer seem to leave the body unprotected. However, punches to the body without thumb protection may be countered by bringing down the elbow for a "late" block and breaking the thumb and/or spraining the wrist.

The Gods of Boxing

Boxing from 520 B.C. to 500 B.C.

"Not even the mighty Polydeukes or the iron son of Alkmene [Herakles] could hold up their hands against him."

-Simonides of Kos, *Epigram for Glaukos*

521 B.C.: Glaukos [*Gray-fish*] of Karystos, son of the farmer Demylos, fixes his father's broken plow, by beating the bent plow-blade back into shape with his hand. Seeing this, Demylos makes hasty preparations to enter his boy in the boxing at the upcoming 65th Olympiad.

520 B.C.: The 65th Olympiad sees the introduction of the men's race in armor, and the entry of the large unschooled farm-boy Glaukos in the boxing for boys. Glaukos won but was cut up in the first bouts by his more skilled opponents. When he was boxing for the crown in the final bout [probably his third] he appeared to be on the verge of fainting from blood-loss, when his father called out, "Son, the plough-touch." Glaukos responded by hammering [probably literally] his opponent with a knockout blow [most likely as he shifted into a right lead].

519 B.C.: Glaukos is victorious in the men's boxing at Nemea.

518 B.C.: Glaukos is victorious in boxing at the Isthmian agon and in the 15th Pythiad.

517 B.C.: Glaukos wins the boxing at the Nemean agon.

516 B.C.: Glaukos is victorious at the Isthmus, and does not finish or perhaps does not enter the 66th Olympiad. This Olympiad should have been Glaukos'. One senses that there must have been a nemesis, a man that Glaukos met and could not defeat at Olympia, but who failed to enter those other contests at which Glaukos was victorious. In fact, as Glaukos was known to have become the most skilled boxer of his time, his nemesis must have been vested with some natural attributes, that would have made him legendary.

Does a look through the chronicles of Pausanias reveal a legendary boxer with nothing but an Olympic victory?

A likely candidate is Damarkhus [*Submission-ruler*] of Parrhasia, a small town in mountainous Arkadia, who was reputed to have lived as a werewolf for nine years! Pausanias warns us not to believe the tale of Damarkhus. But perhaps Damarkhus suffered from some ailment or simply became a recluse or hermit for some years following his active fighting years—a mode of behavior commonly attributed to legendary Chinese and Japanese martial artists. Perhaps he was simply a shepherd who secluded himself for the nine years—the typical two Olympiad campaign span of a dominant ancient boxer—of his athletic career and ran with his dogs over the mountain paths for exercise?

515 B.C.: Glaukos is victorious at Nemea.

514 B.C.: Glaukos is victorious at the Isthmus and at the 16th Pythiad.

513 B.C.: Glaukos is victorious at Nemea.

512 B.C.: Glaukos is victorious at the Isthmus and fails to enter, or perhaps is defeated, at the 67th Olympiad. As Glaukos fails to win any Olympiads as an adult and does not finish another Pythiad despite dominating the Nemean and Isthmian agons. One should look for another possible rival.

Epitherses [?] son of Metrodorus of Erythrae, was credited with winning two Olympiads and two Pythiads, as well as one each at Nemea and the Isthmus. Epitherses record suggests that he fought at the end of Glaukos' career; and that Glaukos was either unbeatable at the lesser agons, or that Epitherses simply didn't enter those contests.

Note: Glaukos may have been banned by the Olympic judges from future competition due to the ugly fashion in which he won as a boy, which, according to one account, had displeased the crowd.

511 & 510 B.C.: Glaukos wins at Nemea and the Isthmus.

509 & 508 B.C.: Glaukos wins at Nemea and the Isthmus. The political reforms of Kliesthenes are instituted in Athens.

507 & 506 B.C.: Glaukos wins at Nemea and the Isthmus

505 & 504 B.C.: Glaukos wins boxing at Nemea and the Isthmus and retires. As with other legendary boxers of this era he was later said to be favored by the gods, being a son of Glaukos the minor sea-spirit.

C. 500 B.C.: Nikokles [*Victory's-Honor*] of Aegina wins the boxing crown at the Isthmus. He may have been a descendent of Praxidamas. Themistius [?] of Aegina wins the boxing and the pankration at Epidauros, being the first known fighter to even attempt such a double victory. It is likely that the relatively new practice of high-handedness which served the wrestler Timasitheon [See *All-Power-Fighting*] and the boxer Glaukos so well now made it possible for a boxer to challenge a pankratiast.

The Gods of Boxing

Figure 52-A.
Getting Caught in a Long Shift
From a 6th Century B.C. Greek vase of uncertain date

    The orthodox boxer on the left has posted a right jab, which has caught his opponent shifting from a left lead to a right lead in order to land a hammer-fist [which remains half executed]. As the shifting fighter's left knee buckles, the stronger fighter steps on his thigh with his left foot in order to push him down, where he will pound him out with the right uppercut he has chambered.

    Shifting is a tactic that is most useful as a deft ruse [such as the solar plexus punch of Robert Fitzsimmons which he employed in the 1890s] or to maintain momentum when hunting an opponent on the run [such as the straight right followed by a right jab to corner a rightward drifting mover, that was successfully employed by "Marvelous" Marvin Hagler in the 1980s]. Poorly schooled fighters that shift out of desperation tend to eat very hard jabs and will generally be knocked out.

Figure 52-B
Working the Right Uppercut off of the posted Jab
From a tracing of uncertain origin, in the style typical of late 6th Century Athenian art

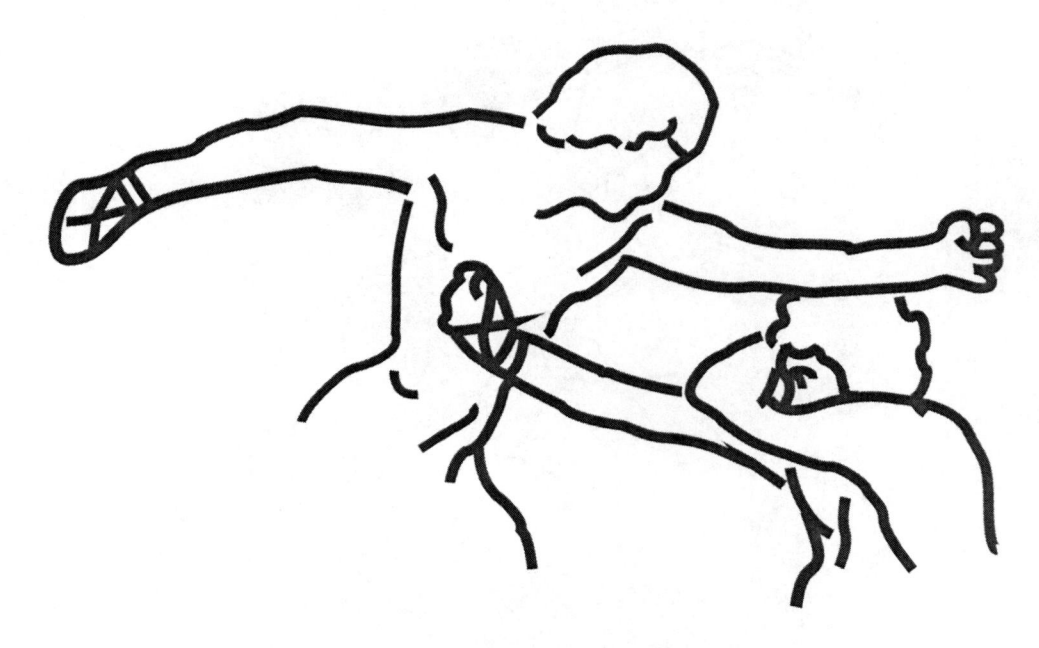

   The aggressor to the left had either missed a hard left jab because the opponent slipped or ducked the blow, or he is following up a glancing blow by forcing his opponent down with his forearm. The opponent is making a weak attempt at body punching from his poor leverage position as he covers up with the left cross-arm guard also seen in Figure 64. Both fighters in this piece have only their right hand wrapped for power punching, and appear to be guarding and jabbing with the left. The aggressor is already chambered for a vicious uppercut to the chin, and appears to be well on his way to finishing the fight.

The Gods of Boxing

Figure 53.
Passing at Uppercut Range
From a Greek vase of the late 6th Century

    The leftward fighter is maintaining a very high guard and has apparently just slipped a straight right. His high lead may represent a passive guard or simply the terminus of a missed lead hand uppercut. His right hand is chambered in the classic Greek position ready to deliver a hammer-fist, uppercut, or plunging straight punch to the heart. His opponent to the right may be shifting after a missed jab. However, it is also possible that he is simply reaching into his bag of fistic tricks for a left-handed hammer-fist or uppercut in an attempt to stop his opponent [who has already passed his right hand] from turning in and tearing up his exposed left side.

Figure 54.
The Sway-Back Defense
From an Attic hydra, 520 B.C.

　　The fighter on the left was stepping in with a one-two combination when the shorter fighter to the right posted a vicious jab between his hands which has split open his nose. While his nose gushes blood the taller fighter leans back at the waist and keeps his fists out in front to ward off the smaller fighter, who appears eager to throw his right hand.
　　Like the fighters from the Archaic period, these boxers of the early Classical period tend to post the jab with a long step, which probably made such disasters rather common. A fight fan of this period would see a lot of KOs coming via the hard left jab.
　　The rightmost fighter is in a right lead. This could be read as a shift. However, the chambered rear left hand makes this appear to be a true right lead.

Figure 55.
Pipe-Player & Bye-sitter at Competition
From the Attic hydra featured in Figure 54.

The double-flute player is providing the rhythm for the ongoing fights, which appear to have been held simultaneously without separate officials for each bout. The flute player would be the winner of the musical competition that opened this agon. At such agons that had no musical events, the most famous musical victors available would most likely be retained to pipe for the prize-fighters and jumpers.

The man adjusting his wraps at the foot of the piper has drawn a bye, and is preparing to draw lots with the winners of the two ongoing bouts for the semi-final bout. If he draws another bye he will be matched fresh against an exhausted fighter for the final bout.

Figure 56.
The Elbow Guard
From the Attic hydra featured in Figures 54 & 55.

Again, the larger fighter in this bout has eaten a posted jab and is bleeding heavily from the nose. He appears to be shielding his face with his right elbow as he leans back. This isn't as much of a disaster as that depicted in Figure 54, as the smaller fighter on the left is going to have some trouble getting past the right fist of the larger man, and, if he ducks into the left, might get caught with a plunging hammer-fist.

Whoever survives this bout is going to have a tough time winning the event if they don't draw the next bye. All thing considered this agon offered a very entertaining fight card.

Figure 57-A.
Posting the Bare-knuckle Jab
From a PanAthenaic vase, 515 B.C.

Both boxers are in an orthodox stance at very close range, with the judge to the left and a gesticulating trainer to the right, who appears to be scolding the losing fighter.

The fighter to the right has missed with a right uppercut. The other fighter has avoided the blow by some means [most likely by drawing his head back] and has countered with a vicious posted jab which is connecting to the chin. The rightmost fighter is well on his way to his back and is breaking his fall with his left hand.

As these boxers are bare knuckle fighters it may be that this illustration represents a pankration match. If so, than the fallen fighter might expect the following treatment by his adversary...

"Leaping very high,
I stomp down
My foot dropping
Heavily..."
 -Askhylos, *Eumenides*

If, however, this represents an unconventional boxing bout for which the boxers did not wrap their hands, than the downed fighter could expect his opponent to hover over him as he tried to rise, raining down hammer blows and plunging knuckle punches to the neck, collarbone and back, as well as uppercuts to the face.

The second on the right may be signaling for the bout to be ended. The judge looks on with an open hand and stayed rod, indicating that he does not concur.

Note: Figure B in this set, while a work crafted by a different hand, presents the likely terminus of the action in Figure A.

Figure 57 B.
The Finish
From an Attic amphora, c 520 B.C.

The downed fighter in this scene has assumed the very posture that could have been expected of the falling fighter in Figure 57-A. While the dominant fighter steps on his right lower leg with his lead left foot and digs a left hook to the back while readying a vicious right uppercut, the fallen fighter has turned to the second [or assistant judge?] and signaled his submission by raising his left index finger for the second to see. The second is relaying the sign of submission to the judge. The judge appears to be concurring by touching the thumb and small finger of his upturned left hand as he prepares to bring down the forks of his rod on the back of the victor.

These two figures taken together represent an excellent study of the decorum of victory and defeat observed by the loser, second, judge, and victor, in that order.

Figure 58.
Fighting in the Clinch
From a black-figured Attic stamnos, c.520 B.C.

These athletes are belted after the old Homeric fashion. This may represent an Athenian attempt to reintroduce the athletic belt, or may simply represent foreign athletes or the heroes of literature. This piece is also unconventional for the period in that the leftmost fighter is clinching and is not being punished by a judge. This fact may indicate that clinching with the hands was banned and that arm hooking was not, or, it may represent a pankration bout, or a bout between non-Greeks who did not box according to Greek tradition. In any case, this is an interesting scene possibly representing an agon or a training session. An agon is the more likely setting.

The Gods of Boxing

The rightmost fighter has missed a strong jab and his opponent has under-hooked the jabbing arm with his own left and is about to deliver a straight right to the heart or a hook to the kidney. In the meantime, the fighter is eating straight right arm punches to the face, and his nose is dripping a great deal of blood. Since the fighters' lead feet have passed at this range than the boxer who first steps out to his right will gain the tactical advantage.

Figure 59.
The Open-Hand Style
From an Attic cup, 515 B.C.

These two boxers represent an evolution of the heavy-handed archaic style of boxing. While the technique of the standing boxer is reminiscent of that used by the boxer wearing only one thong in Figure 37, it indicates a stylistic departure from both the one-handed and heavy-handed schools of boxing of the archaic period, and is more in line with the vital-point school of thought demonstrated by finger-jabbing and thumb-jabbing among earlier Greek and Egyptian boxers.

Wrapping the wrist exclusively indicates an increase in straight power punching and a decrease in hooking, hammer-fisting and uppercutting. The lead palm is a feeler to insure accurate punching and the wrapped wrist will support the wrist against the force of such blows that may often have been sunk to the body, thus putting the fist in danger of being wrenched or of being caught by an elbow brought down too late to protect the body. The wrapped wrist suggests aggressive empty hand tactics and linear power punching to soft targets [like the body, eyes and nose] opened up by these empty-hand techniques; supported by a passive high guard with the wrapped wrist protecting the face and the elbows being brought down to attack the extended arm of a body-puncher. Hammer punches might still be delivered to the neck, collar bone and arm, but not to the skull. The high incidence of downward hammer punches might explain the rarity of ducking under hook punches, as such bobbing tactics would put the boxer at a high risk of injury to his neck and collar bone—a bone which is easily broken.

The unmarked loser in this illustration appears to be quitting; simply surrendering to a better fighter without putting up much of a struggle. Such gutless opponents were undoubtedly plentiful. In a society where a majority of the young men boxed at some level one would expect a higher incidence of emotionally unfit boxers at lower levels of competition, than in the modern world where only a few choose the risks of boxing. As this illustration depicts youthful fighters, it most likely represents the local Athenian event.

Figure 60.
Early High-Handedness
From a PanAthenaic amphora c.515 B.C.

This is a transitional piece, depicting an old heavy-hand stylist against a practitioner of the new style of high-handedness. The heavy-hand stylist on the left has stepped too long to bring his rear right fist to bear. The fighter to the right is fading from a shorter base with an eye jab already on the way. This will probably be trapped by the advancing fighter, who will bring his lead in against his opponent's upper forearm, and then probably get speared, palmed or punched by the rightmost fighter who is already set to punch over the shorter man's lead.

These two styles illustrate the evolution of Glaukos, who began as an unskilled boy fighting in the style demonstrated by the leftmost fighter, and attained fame and finished a long successful career fighting in the new style demonstrated by the fighter on the right. The open hand style of high-handedness resembles some forms of Chinese boxing from the waist up, although the footwork is reminiscent of early 20th century gloved boxing as practiced by Robert Fitzsimmons and Jack Johnson.

The judge on the right is quite pleased with the proceedings as he has not deployed his staff or rod. The trainer on the left, as is usual, hold a pair of hand straps, perhaps to re-wrap his man's hands should he win, or to prepare himself or another fighter for the next bout. Perhaps he is on duty with spare hand-straps in-case one fighter's wraps become undone and must be replaced in mid-bout?

Figure 61.
In-fighting with High-hands
From an Attic hydra c.515 B.C.

The fighter on the left is trapping his opponent's right palm thrust with his left and is attempting to score with his own right palm. Unfortunately, he has walked into a late lead palm thrust by his opponent, who has his rear foot out at 90 degrees and is holding his ground as he drives his palm up into the advancing fighter's nose. The fighter on the right has a shorter base—not having stepped in so long as the leftmost fighter—and is in a good position to capitalize on his jolting lead, which will produce a lot of blood. Expect a swift finish in this bout as the right most fighter steps to his right and plants a straight right or uppercut to his dazed opponent's chin.

The Gods of Boxing

Figure 62.
Getting Punished in the Clinch
From a PanAthenaic amphora, c.510 B.C.

The fighter to the left has apparently shifted into a right lead to catch up with a shifty left-hander. He has under-hooked the extended right lead of his opponent at the shoulder joint and is whacking away with lateral hammer-fists to the ear and/or uppercuts to the body and chin. The fighter on the right is attempting to cover with a high guard without much success. However, the judge is seeing things his way and is already laying into the beastly broad aggressor, who will most likely continue to break the rules until the judge's forked willow rod convinces him to desist. Should he knockout his opponent he will either be barred from further rounds of competition, or, if this bout is for the prize, than the prize will be dedicated to his opponent or to the god or hero for whom the agon is being held.

Figure 63.
Gym Rats up to No-Good
From an Athenian marble base, flip-side of Figure 51*. c.510 B.C.

These young men are having a wager over a dog verses cat fight as their friends look on. This is the kind of stuff that went on in the back of the classical palaestra in the boys' club room. Take note of the lightweight and mobile looking seats, and the fact that all four of the boys carry sticks. This should give a good indication of the nature of the entourages that accompanied fighters to major agons. With visors instead of sunglasses and castanets and double-flutes instead of boom-boxes, one would find little other than the clothing to differentiate these Athenian boys, who might have accompanied Melissius to his pankration meets, than the wannabe gangster rappers that accompany 21st Century prize-fighters to their bouts.

The figure on the far right appears to be an elder; perhaps the Rock Newman [an obnoxious 1990's manager of heavyweight contender and champion Riddick Bowe] of his day.

*The third volume, *All-Power-Fighting*.

Figure 64.
Cover & Quit
From an Attic kylix, c.510 B.C.

The boxer on the right is an orthodox fighter who has stepped around the lead right of his left-handed opponent and has driven at least one hard right down the middle. He has thrown a hard jab which has been blocked and is chambering a "bolo" type uppercut with his wrapped right fist—the only one of the four hands depicted being wrapped. The fighter on the left is going down due to the buckling of his rear left leg, which has probably buckled from the force of a hard straight right to the chin. He is covering his eyes—the orbits of which could be terribly damaged by the wrapped right fist of his opponent—with his elbow and his right ear with his wrist. Of course he can see that he's about to eat another crunching right, so he signals his submission by raising his right hand and extending his index finger.

This is yet another use of the cross-arm guard among boxers without their left hand wrapped. This is certainly the ancient Greek equivalent of the "peek-a-boo" guard used by Floyd Patterson in the 1950s and 1960s.

The fighters in this illustration appear to be middleweights or cruiserweights of the youth class of intermediate fighters between boyhood and manhood. There was no such class at Olympia, but this was a common class of competitor at local festivals such as the PanAthenae.

The Gods of Boxing

Boxing From 496 to 485 B.C.

"Last of heroes is Kleomedes [*Lion-of-Persia*] of Astypalaea;
   Honor him with sacrifices as an immortal."
   -*Pythian Oracle*

496 B.C.: At the 71st Olympiad Kleomedes met Ikkos [?] of Epidauros in the final round of boxing. The bout resulted in the death of Ikkos, and the judges convicted Kleomedes of intentionally killing Ikkos. This means that Ikkos must have been killed in a clinch, or was gouged, bitten, stomped, or punched after having submitted. The crown would have been dedicated to Zeus and Kleomedes was fined 4 talents. Kleomedes returned home in grief and pulled down the pillar of a school house, causing the roof to collapse on the 60 children within. His fellow citizens stoned the boxer, who ran and hid in the Temple of Athena. He was suspected of hiding himself in a chest. But when it was broken open he was not within. Envoys were sent to Delphi to consult the Pythian Oracle. The priestess, who sat over a fissure that released nature gas and caused her to have visions, informed the envoys that Kleomedes was no longer among the living and should be propitiated as a hero.

The Astypalaeans continued to sacrifice to Kleomedes for at least 600 years. However, this author suspects that Kleomedes made his way into exile in Persia, where Greek athletes seem to have been welcome guests. Perhaps he lived with characters such as Timokreon and his criminal associates?

A similar fate awaited Diognetes [*Heavenly-?*] of Krete who, after killing his opponent in boxing at Olympia on some uncertain date, was denied the crown and forced to live in exile. However, he too was ultimately honored as a hero.

494 B.C.: The Persians crush the revolt of the Asian Greeks, at a time when Timokreon and Kleomedes, both citizens of Greek Islands adjacent to Greek Asia, were probably living in exile in the vicinity.

492 B.C.: Philon [*Beloved*], son of Glaukos of Karystos, was victorious in boxing at the 72nd Olympiad. On the island of Thasos, the nine-year old boy Theogenes [*God-born*], son of Timosthenes, the local priest of Herakles, picks up the statue of a god in the local market place and carries it home. The citizens want to kill the boy for this sacrilege, but listen instead to an elder, and make Theogenes carry the statue back to the market. From this day on Theogenes is famed across Greece for his strength.

The Gods of Boxing

491 B.C.: Gelon, a major player in Olympic chariot racing, becomes Tyrant of Gela in Sicily.

490 B.C.: Glaukos of Karystos is appointed governor of Kamerina in Sicily by Gelon.

Timokreon [*Esteemed-Butcher*] of Rhodes is an undistinguished pentathlete who is ostracized by his fellow Rhodians. During his exile he was patronized by another exile by the name of Themistokles, who was an innkeeper, thief, loan-shark and hitman, who eventually committed suicide. Timokreon apparently worked as a butcher or hitman at Themistokles' inn, and spent some time as a drinking companion, informer, and entertainer among the fabulously rich Persian elite. Invited to the court of the Persian King [probably Darius I] for a feast, Timokreon impressed the King of Kings by eating and drinking more than anyone thought possible. The day after the feast Timokreon fought seven boxing exhibitions against Persian fighters, scoring seven KOs. He then began shadow-boxing. When the King asked why he was doing this, Timokreon responded, "Because I still have an equal number of knock-out punches for anyone willing to face me." After his death Timokreon was immortalized in the following epitaph, composed by the famous Persian-hating poet, Simonides of Kos...

"Having eaten much, drunk much, and speaking Insults of many men, here lies Esteemed-Butcher of Rhodes."

489 B.C.: Glaukos is killed during an armed revolt at Kamerina. Some ancient writers believed that Glaukos had been set up as a scapegoat by Gelon, and that it was ultimately through treachery from above that he perished. He was buried by the Karystians on a small island that was renamed the Isle of Glaukos. His son apparently adopted Korkyra as his homeland. Such transference of primary citizenship was not unknown among the widely traveled athletic class. In fact, the people of Anthedon in Boeotia later claimed that Glaukos was their most famous son, and that Karystos was his adopted homeland.

488 B.C.: Philon is victorious in the boxing at the 73rd Olympiad. Having accomplished what his father had not—gathering 2 Olympic crowns—and having become an influential citizen of one of the wealthiest of the Greek states, Philon has a statue of himself erected in the Altis at Olympia next to the chariot of Gelon, who had won the race on that year, and may or may not have been Gelon the Tyrant. Next to the statue of Philon stands the likeness of Agametor of Mantineia who defeated the boys in boxing, and next to him

Philon has a statue of his father erected, depicting him sparring in his famous high-handed boxing style. Simonides, the foremost epigrapher of the day, composes the inscription carved onto the base of the statues of Philon and his father. The epigram for Glaukos compares him favorably with the prize-fighting gods Polydeukes and Herakles. The epigram for Philon reads:

"My fatherland is Korkyra, Philon; I am—son of Glaukos
Twice I took victory by fist at the Olympiads"

487 B.C.: War between Athens and Aegina.
486 B.C.: Pindar writes the 7th Pythian ode.
485 B.C.: Pythogoras of Samos puts the boxing knowledge of his forefathers to work training the young prospect Euthymos [*Grace-speaker*] of Lokri for the upcoming 74th Olympiad.

Figure 65-A.
High-Handedness
From a PanAthenaic? amphora, 500 B.C.

This appears to depict a sparring session officiated by a trainer who is armed with a willow switch for enforcing discipline and a staff, which may have been a coaching aid; perhaps being used as a prod, a temporary barrier, or simply an extension of the coaching hand to remind a fighter of posture flaws from a safe distance without the need to stop the action.

The rightmost fighter has posted a vertical jab which may not land, as his opponent is attempting to trap that forearm and is timing his rush well, necessitating the odd posture he has adopted. The jabbing fighter is fading back over his right knee and is squaring his stance which leaves him in a vulnerable position against his shorter and heavier opponent. If he plants that jab between the eyes as he straightens the rear leg he might stop the other's advance. Failing that, he might salvage the situation by pivoting off his lead left foot as he bends his left elbow and foils the right-handed trap attempt by rolling his left arm over from the shoulder. Such a pivot would narrow his stance and possibly set the opponent off balance. Another option would be to take a short step to the right and draw in the left foot while pressing down on the shorter fighter's shoulder or upper arm with the right hand. This draw step to the right would be beyond the ability of the average fighter of any period. However, if successful, would place the opponent in a terribly vulnerable position with only one hand to defend against two.

The fighter on the left could improve his position by drawing up his rear leg halfway and taking a step in between the legs of his fading opponent. His taller opponent seems very evasive so he should keep up the pressure and stay close. It is unclear what type of blow he is likely to throw, though a palm thrust or finger jab with the right hand to the opponent's eye would require no additional positioning. Defensively, he needs to slip his head to the outside of the opponent's left fist and keep his left guard high to shield against an overhand right, which appears that it might be his opponent's most likely counterpunch.

The Gods of Boxing

Figure 65-B
High-handedness on the Outside
Greek vase of uncertain date

   These fighters appear to be sparring for position on the outside, and could possibly be all-power-fighters boxing at kicking range. This may be a bare-knuckle boxing bout, as high-handed boxers would face the problem of their wraps unraveling. Or, this might be the later stages of a bout during which the wraps unraveled and fell away.

The Gods of Boxing

Figure 66.
Illyrian Boxers
From a bronze engraving, early 5th Century

These two fighters appear to be engaged in a bout fought with dumbbells. Or perhaps they are simply warming up with dumbbells before boxing over the trophy, which appears to be a helmet with stand accompanied by a spear—the arms of a warrior. Robed figures wearing hats look on from the right. If the boxers are fighting with some type of dumbbell than these were probably fashioned of wood and or leather. There is no reason to suppose some kind of gruesome metal weapon. The jab of the right most fighter is pronated while the jab of the left fighter is hyperpronated. Both have chambered their rear hand to deliver a swinging uppercut. A hook or overhand right with the rear hand would be theoretically possible, however unlikely, since both punches would endanger the puncher's shoulder, and the reaching uppercut was a popular blow in this period.

With dumbbell boxers we must accept the possibility that these fighters might have just been using the weights to warm up before a bout, like a baseball player on deck with a weight on his bat.

Figure 67.
Etruscan Hammer-Fist
From a wall-painting from Tomba delle Bighe, Tarquinia, c. 500 B.C.
From the same wall painting as Figures 25 & 68.

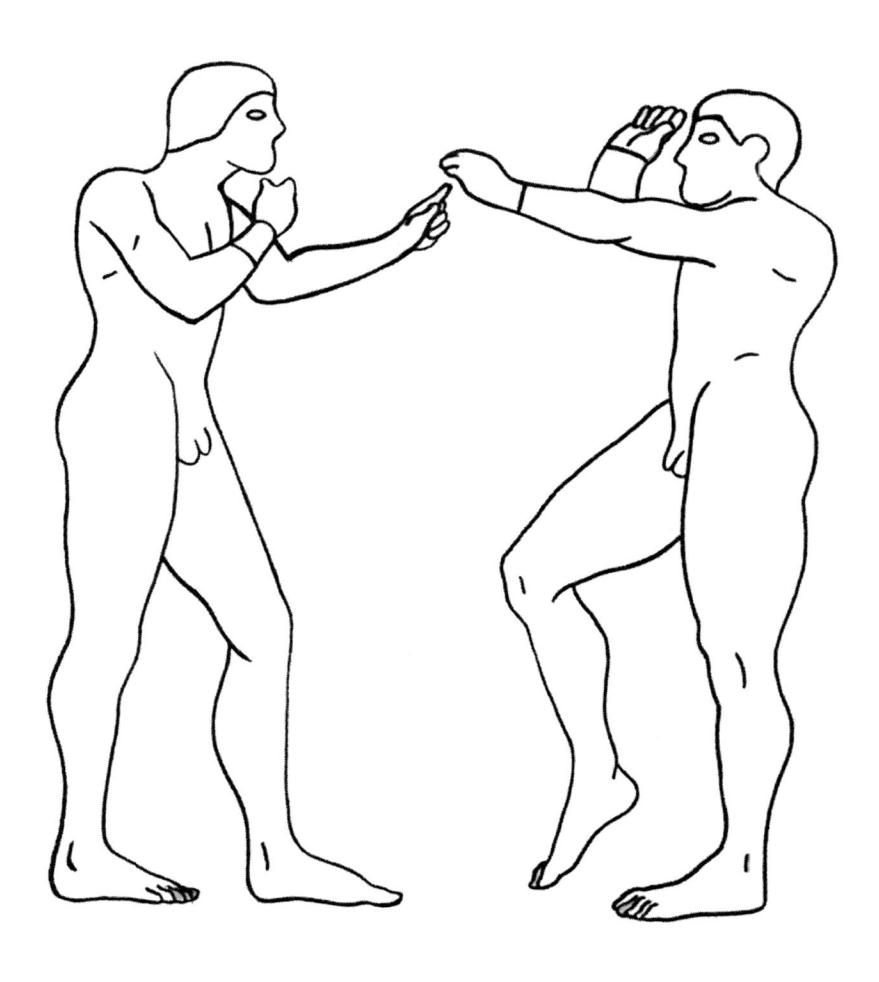

    The boxer on the left is maintaining a very modern looking guard. However, his feet are flat-footed, which is the primary difference between Greek and Etruscan boxers. All of the Etruscan boxers—though not the wrestlers and pankratiasts—are entirely flat footed. The flat-footedness may be a copyist's error, as Gardiner claims the Etruscan athletic paintings were copies of Greek origins. But this author suspects that Etruscan artists depicted boxers, based on Greek originals or Etruscan models, as boxing flat-footed precisely because they did just that. The hands on these fighters are much more heavily wrapped than the hands on Greek boxers depicted on Greek vases from the same period.

The fighter on the right has led with a vertical left jab and is now shifting his right leg into the lead to gain the reach and the gravitational force to land an effective hammer-fist. The fleshy bottom edge of his fist should come down on his opponent's bicep or collarbone as his foot plants heel first just to the outside of the opponent's lead foot. Though not a knockout blow, the vertical hammer-fist is very painful and partially disabling if landed on the collarbone or bicep.

Figure 68.
Etruscan High-Handedness
From the wall-painting from Tomba delle Bighe, Tarquina, featured in Figures 25 & 67, c.500 B.C.

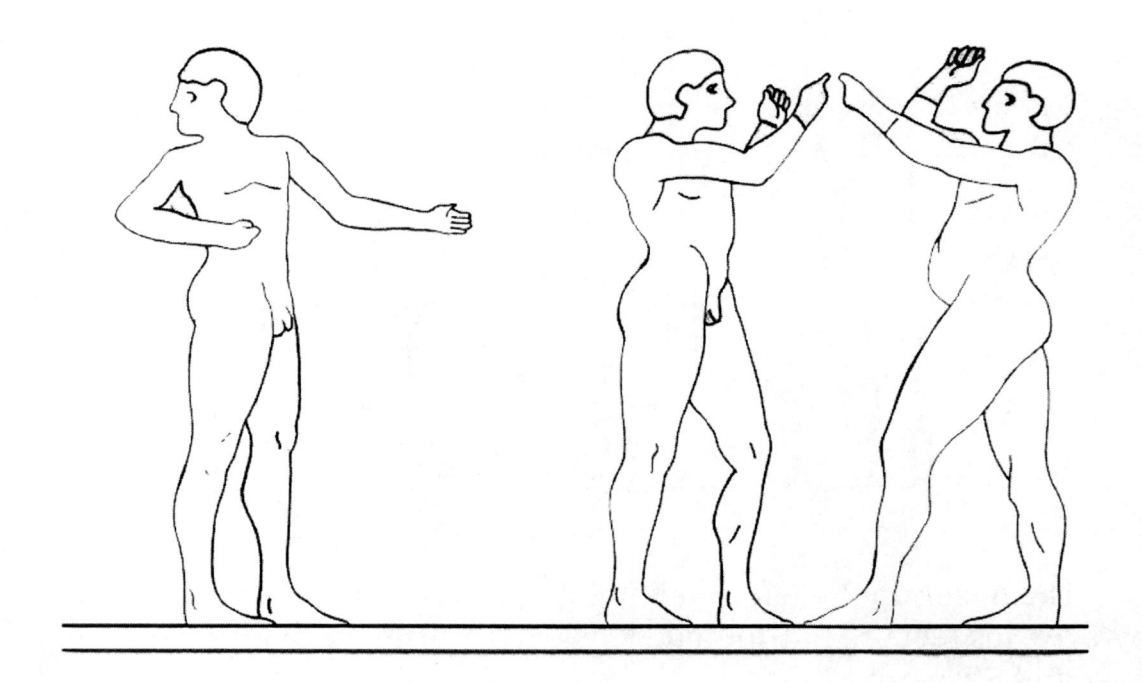

These figures are flat-footed and their torsos are already rotated forward, leaving them in a poor position to throw the straight right. Their power option seems to be the downward hammer-fist, which the fighter on the right is chambered to throw as the second part of a combination, the first part of which—a vertical left jab—has already been blocked by his opponent's right guard. It appears that the fighter on the left has used the same portion of his fist to block with—the outside palm—as his opponent is prepared to hammer with. From the positions depicted I would expect this exchange to go on for a while, with the rightmost fighter hammering at his opponent's guard with his right in hopes of slipping in a left jab to the face, which could set up a shift into a right lead accompanied by a downward chop to the face, neck or collarbone. Overall this looks less entertaining than the fight depicted in Figure 67.

Figure 69.
The Barrier
From a Black-figure PanAthenaic amphora by Kleophrades, c.490 B.C.

This is a beautiful piece of art. It also depicts more completely than other pieces the character of Classical Greek boxing. In the foreground are two bearded assistants of the judge who stands to the right. They are depicted as being child-sized despite being bearded and nearer. Were they dwarves? Or were they intentionally depicted as being small because they represented non-athletes that deserved less attention than the fighters and officials of the athletic class? The pole held between these two figures served to keep the fighters from moving too much. It was probably made of ash or cornel wood. Authors of late antiquity describe a ladder being used for this purpose. It is assumed that such measures were only taken to confine the fighters when one or both were apt to move so much that the judges feared there would be no resolution.

For the most part a staff held by a single judge would suffice to remind the fighters to stay on the dug up area. In fact, the author's experience fighting barefoot on dug up earth, demonstrated that any fighter who was not in danger of imminent KO would avoid stepping off the raked area because of the likelihood of sustaining stone bruises and thorn punctures. Of course, ancient Greek feet were probably quite tough. However, digging into stony ground while pivoting with a punch exposes the bare feet to more stress than simply walking or running. As usual the judge holds his willow switch and purple robe of office. The willow switch used by the judge is similar in appearance to the sticks used by harvesters to whip the fruit off of the branches of the olive tree. Ironically this amphora would have contained Attic olive oil to be given as a prize to the winner of the mens' boxing contest at the Great PanAthenae. Oil protected and cleansed the exposed skin of the naked athletes and was even more expensive than it is in modern times.

To the left stands a trainer, second, or bye-sitter encouraging one of the fighters. By his body language he appears to be suggesting the delivery of a left uppercut to the chin and a straight right to the body. Of course he might simply be waiting his turn to fight, and is depicted in the process of warming up.

The fighters themselves are fighting in the high-handed fashion of the time. These are large men who are fighting on their toes from the left-hand lead. The fighter to the right has thrown a vertical left jab which his opponent has stopped with a right-handed palm catch. He is following with a palm thrust to the nose, which his opponent has countered with a cut-off punch. A cut-off punch is a closed-fist tactic aimed at the open hand and/or the inside of the attacking arm. The objective is to break the fingers or thumb of the attacking open hand, and, if not successful in actually damaging the hand, to glance the inside of the attacking forearm at such an angle as to cause the attacking arm to be driven out of position to the outside; setting the defender up for a nice shovel-hook with the intercepting fist to the attacker's unguarded face. In Filipino martial arts this is called a "destruction" of the attack.

The author's sense of this fight is that the rail was brought out to pressure the fighter on the left to stand and fight. As a skilled boxer, he would tend to move to his right against his opponent's left lead to avoid the right and get two hands against one, so the pole was obviously employed to corner him. It looks like an even fight at this juncture.

Figure 70.
Athenian Boxers I
From an Attic kilex by Duris, 490 B.C., from the same piece depicted in Figure 71.

A single judge supervises two pairings of fighters with his forked rod. The pair to the left demonstrate perfect high-handed offensive form. The rightward fighter is leaning back on the defensive with his rear foot posted as a break at a 90 degree angle. He has the longer arms and is trying to keep the other fighter at bay with his long jab.

The aggressor is entering with a high-commitment posted vertical jab that is coming up short. His rear hand is chambered with his palm facing out. The three right-handed punches that can be effectively thrown from this guard are: a lateral hammer-fist to kidney, elbow, shoulder or ear at optimum force; a plunging vertical straight right to the heart with moderate efficiency or to the chin with poor efficiency; or a bolo type uppercut that is only good as a finishing blow, as it is too telegraphic. That uppercut could be kept tight to the chest as the fist is supinated and be turned into a vicious uppercut to the chin by thrusting the dropped elbow off of the hip, although these blows are generally depicted with a swinging action demonstrated by the standing fighter in the pair to the right, who has knocked his opponent down with a posted left jab and is finishing him with a vertical fist uppercut, which looks like it is going to land in an attitude similar to a modern karate ridge-hand blow.

It appears that the fighter to the right ate a hard posted jab as he was doing a rightward shift into a hammer-punch. He is maintaining a high right guard and has not signaled submission yet, something which the judge might be pleading with him to do.

Figure 71.
Athenian Boxers II
From the Attic kilex, 480 B.C.

The scenes that accompanied this piece include a fighter strapping his hands [left], and a youth exercising with jumping weights [right], suggesting the use of dumbbells as a training aid for boxers. There is also a youth picking the ground, a youth strapping his hand, an official supervising two wrestlers, and another official supervising a youth preparing to cast a javelin. Gardiner identifies this as a training session rather than an agon, and I am inclined to agree.

The boxing is being closely supervised by the official, who is keeping the right most fighter from stepping out to his right. The aggressive fighter to the left is a southpaw who is getting inside the posted jab of his opponent by using his extended right forearm to deflect the jab. He is chambered for a left hammer-fist or uppercut. The man on the right is chambered for the hammer-fist, straight-right or uppercut.

Figure 72.
Athenian Boxers III
From an Attic cup by the Triptolemos Painter, 490 B.C.

On the right two boxers supervised by an official wrap their hands. Note the tension that the standing boxer is using to apply his hand strap. Leather wraps can be difficult to apply over knuckles and tend to bunch up in reaction to hand flexion. The figures supervising the fighters may be identified as judges, trainers or gymnasiarchs. At competition trainers are sometimes depicted naked. But they apparently go clothed in the training area.

The combatants to the left are head hunting. The rightward fighter is leaning away as he jabs and appears to be attempting to throw a straight right which is being cut off by the more aggressive boxer's strongly posted palm-jab. The fighter to the right looks like he's lining up a straight right hand. The fighter to the left is angling for an uppercut. If either man gets what he wants, someone is going to sleep.

5th Century Training and the Psychology of High-handedness

"Strong of hand, with the spirit of a lion and light of foot."
-Bakhylides, an Epigram for Argeios [?] of Keos, for a Nemean victory in 465 B.C.

One must be careful in assuming the character of Classical boxing on the strength of the surviving art and literature because virtually all of what is left to us in descriptive terms comes from Athens, though virtually none of the Olympic-class champions were Athenians. Athens was to Classical boxing what New York is to modern boxing, and Olympia would therefore be analogous to Las Vegas. With this caution aired, the author thinks it is reasonable to rely on Attic art as an indication of boxing trends because much of it was crafted to commemorate the PanAthenaic agons which were open to all Greeks.

The primary trends that emerge in Classical boxing are complimentary, heavier hitting and a more proactive defense typified by head and body movement and great value placed on having the hands held high, not so much as a guard, but in order to attack the opponent's attack with a controlling slap [parrying with tactile force] in order to attain and maintain the upper-hand. High-handedness as it was called was embraced as a grappling counter-measure against the unbeatable Milo in 516 B.C. and was touted as a training method. In fact, many modern writers have assumed that "high-handedness" was nothing more than an ancient term for sparring, and have translated it literally as light sparring, although this is incorrect and at variance with the clear evolution of the term.

The simple truth about "high-handedness" was that it could be practiced without the practitioners crippling or killing one-another! Any contact art that can be practiced without recourse to artificially imposed behavior [such as the uke factor in karate where one practitioner is the doomed uke who stumbles knowingly into all manner of unlikely and perfect attacks and defenses] without sustaining a real performance-degrading level of damage

The Gods of Boxing

[such as in modern gloved boxing, where as much brain damage occurs in sparring as in competition*]. The one reason why grappling is always practiced at a consistently higher level than striking is that one can have hundreds of wrestling matches with no brain damage, while even 10 boxing bouts routinely causes chronic brain damage to modern amateur boxers. High-handedness—the modern understanding of which is dominated by practitioners of Chinese-boxing, and is known in the U.S. as "trapping"—is a boxing doctrine than can be effectively practiced with limited gear as a form of "slap-boxing" or "touch-boxing", thus offered the early Classical boxer a low-impact form of training that translated directly to a survivable style of defensive boxing, at the same time that punching mechanics were becoming increasingly fearsome.

The rise of high-handedness as a competition and training tool coincided with three related phenomena:

1. The practice of high-handedness and finger breaking among over-matched wrestlers.

2. The dominance of boxers in the pankration, which had, for its first 150 years, been dominated strictly by specialists, with no entry of note by a boxer or wrestler.

3. The presence of hand-ball courts and hand-ball instructors in the palaestra, which was the place where the boxer came to train.

High-handedness as a wrestling tactic is covered in Part III, *All-Power-Fighting*. As one of the primary tactics of the pankration was wrestling the opponent to the ground, the practice of high-handedness as a clinching counter-measure in wrestling would certainly recommend itself to boxers—not trained to "dirty box" in the clinch—who might fancy trying out all that new-fangled punching power in the pankration, which, being the sport of Herakles, god of manliness, was gradually over-taking the pentathlon as the premier venue for the demonstration of all-around athletic ability. As a final note, the hand-ball coach would be a valuable asset to the aspiring trap-boxer.

A trap is a controlling slap best applied with the thumb held snuggly against the forefinger for control and protection of the thumb. When trapping, one is grabbing without using the thumb, utilizing tactile sensitivity. For practice one may experiment with a tennis-ball or lacrosse-ball or golf-ball. Simply play catch at close range by aiming for your partners chin on your toss without using your thumb, and catching the ball on his toss without taking your thumb from its safe position against your forefinger. Do not forget to bend the thumb slightly and cup your fingers. Your trapping ability will benefit greatly.

The Gods of Boxing

Boxing from 484 to 440 B.C.

"Hagesidamos [*Trained-as-subduer*], victor with the fist at Olympia, may offer thanks to Ilas, even as Patroklus did to Akhilles... I have praised the handsome son of Arkhestrsatus, whom, on that day, beside the Olympic altar, I saw take victory by the might of his hands..."
 -Pindar, *Tenth Olympian Ode*, 476 B.C.

484 B.C.: At the 74th Olympiad Euthymus [*Grace-speaker*] of Lokri in Italy wins with the fist.

483 B.C.: Theogenes [*God-born*] of Thasos wins with the fist at Nemea.

482 B.C.: Theogenes wins with the fist at the Isthmus and at the 24th Pythiad.

481 B.C.: Theogenes wins with the fist and in the pankration at Nemea.

480 B.C.: Theogenes wins the boxing and the pankration at the Isthmus. Leonidas and the 300 Spartans fall at Thermopylae [*The Hot Gates*]. At the 75th Olympiad Theogenes enters the boxing and the pankration, defeats Euthymus and is then unable to step up for the final bout in the pankration against Dromeus [*Runner*] of Mantineia. The Eleans fine Theogenes a talent to be dedicated to Zeus for his arrogance and a talent to be paid to Ethymus for his spiteful entry in the boxing. Theogenes pays Ethymus on the spot and agrees not to oppose him at future Olympiads. [...]phanes of Heraia beat the boys in boxing.

479 B.C.: The Greeks defeat the Persians at Plataea, and found various agons in honor of the dead. Theogenes is victorious in the pankration at Nemea and the boxing and pankration at new agons.

478 B.C.: Theogenes wins the boxing at the Isthmus and at the 25th Pythiad.

477 B.C.: Theogenes wins with the fist at Nemea and dominates boxing and pankration at minor agons.

476 B.C.: Theogenes wins with the fist at the Isthmus. At the 76th Olympiad Hegesidamos of Lokri beats the boys with the fist, Ethymus of Lokri beats the men with the fist; Theogenes defeats the men in the pankration and pays his debt to Zeus, a Zane [a statue of Zeus reminding mortals of Theogenes' shame as an oath-breaker] is raised with the fine money at the gateway from the Altis to the stadium, and Pindar writes his *First Olympian Ode*.

The Gods of Boxing

475 B.C.: Theogenes wins the boxing at Nemea and continues to terrorize local athletes at minor agons.

474 B.C.: Theogenes is victorous in boxing at the Isthmus and at the 26th Pythiad.

473 B.C.: Theogenes wins with the fist at Nemea and continues his off-year reign of terror at local agons, comparable to the modern heavyweight world champion showing up at toughman contests and police athletic league amateur bouts—the best pro heavyweight challenging local amateur middleweights!

472 B.C.: Theogenes wins the boxing at the Isthmus and sees a pankratiast who will be unbeatable...

At the 77th Olympiad, Tellon [?] of Mainalos beats the boys in boxing, Euthymus takes his 3rd boxing crown, and Kallias [*Beautiful*] of Athens wins the pankration—if Theogenes entered the pankration is unknown. Pythagoras of Region raised a statue for Euthymus. After his return to Lokri in Italy Euthymus travels to Temesa and rescues a young virgin who was being sacrificed to a local hero [who sounds a lot like a modern serial killer operating under the protection of the local church] by defeating the fiend in a fight. Euthymus will become famous and loved throughout the Greek-speaking world for this act, which freed the people from a terrorizing burden and resulted in his marriage to the young girl.

471 B.C.: In the mean-time Theogenes is still crushing second-rate boxers at Nemea and minor agons. The future playwright Euripides of Athens wins the boy's boxing at the Eleusinian agon.

470 B.C.: Theogenes wins with the fist at the Isthmus and enters the long foot-race at the 27th Pythiad, easily defeating the other entrants—the only evidence we have that ancient boxers ran for conditioning.

Theogenes is the archetype of the overreaching athlete. Had he not tried to take the fist and all-out-fighting at the same Olympiad, he would not have been barred from expressing his desire to be the best boxer at the next three Olympiads, and Euthymus, the mythic Icon, would have been but a footnote in his story.

The hardest aspect of Theogenes' story to swallow is the 1400 victories with which he is credited. This is a ridiculous number considering the logistical difficulties of the times, and probably reflects the habit ancient Greek writers had of adding an extra zero to already large numbers for emphasis. 140 agon victories, with zero to four fights per agon, is believable for Theogenes to have attained in his quest to match the Olympic *quality* that his youthful ambition had denied him with the *quantity* of a long almost superhuman boxing career. It was believed that Theogenes chose to give up combat sports for running at Delphi in order to emulate Achilles who was reputed to have been the swiftest runner among men and had been the lord of Thessaly, just to the north of Delphi. There was even a legend concerning the origins of the Pythian Oracle at Delphi being tied to a son of Achilles who was said to have been slain at Delphi after the fall of Troy.

In the absence of Theogenes among the boxers, Skopadae of Krannon wins boxing and commissions Simonides to write an ode. At the victory feast Skopadae only pays one third the agreed price because two thirds of the poem praised the gods Polydeukes and Kastor. After Simonides leaves the feast the building's roof collapses, killing all. Legend has it that Simonides was saved from the collapse by the gods he praised. But it seems to modern eyes that Skopadae must have been just as stingy in his dealings with the builder of his banquet hall as he was with the poet he hired to immortalize him.

469 B.C.: Theogenes wins with the fist at Nemea.

468 B.C.: Theogenes wins with the fist at the Isthmus. At the 78th Olympiad the agon is extended from 3 to 5 days, a boy from Tyrins wins with the fist, and Menalkes [?] of Opus beats the men with the fist. Simonides dies of old age.

467 B.C.: Theogenes wins with the fist at Nemea. Argos destroys the city of Tyrins.

466 B.C.: Theogenes wins with the fist at the Isthmus, in his [probably] last year of competition.

465 B.C.: Thasos revolts against Athens. Diagoras [*Two-gatherings*] of Rhodes wins boxing at Nemea.

464 B.C.: At the 79th Olympiad Diagoras wins his only Olympic crown, though he will go on to a long career built on victories at lesser agons. He is greatly admired and will father the greatest family of athletes the world will ever know. Pindar later revels in the task of summarizing his accomplishments...

"...so I may honor [Diagoras], for his fairness in combat and his skill with the fist, that giant man who won the crown beside the Alpheus [the river that borders Olympia]...they [the family of Diagoras] surpassed all mortal men by their skill with the hand... With flowers from that contest [at Rhodes] twice has he crowned himself; and thrice at Nemea and rocky Athens; and having won the bronze shield of Argos, and the fine prizes of Arkadia and Thebes, and the agons of Boeotia and Pellana, and at Aegina and Megara where each he was six times victorious...Zeus...grant honor to the hymn ordained for an Olympian victor, and to a hero famed for his fists..."

-Pindar, *Seventh Olympian Ode*, 464 B.C.

463 B.C.: The surrender of Thasos on this year would have enabled Theogenes to return home, in the event that he had been caught touring abroad when hostilities broke out. It is not known what part if any he played in the insurrection against Athens. However, he was remembered after his death as a public benefactor. So it is likely that he used his personal fortune to help rebuild his homeland.

460 B.C.: At the 80th Olympiad Kyniskos [*Dog-victor*] of Mantinae beats the boys with the fist.

459 B.C.: Argos usurps the Nemean games from Kleonae.

456 B.C.: Dromeus [*Runner*] of Stymphalus, two-time Olympian runner, introduces meat diet for athletes.

449 B.C.: Herodotus, father of history, witnesses boxing matches in the delta region of Egypt.

448 B.C.: At the 83rd Olympiad Alkaentos of Leaprus wins the boy's boxing; Diagoras enters as a boxer and as a pankratiast. He loses to his son Akousilaos [*Hearer-of-the-people*] in the boxing, and goes on to the last round of the pankration where he loses to his other son Damagetus [*Subdual-unwilling?*]. The two sons, on defeating their father, carry him on their shoulders through the crowd, who pelts him with flowers and congratulates him on his sons. Diagoras is supposedly the descendent of a princess of Messene who fled from Spartan occupation in the 600s B.C. His name and those of his sons indicate that they were leading citizens of Rhodes. [See the life of Dorieus below.]

444 B.C.: At the 84th Olympiad Herodotus reads from his history and Alkaentos [?] wins the men's boxing

443 B.C.: The colony of Thurii is founded on the site of the ruins of Sybaris in Greek Italy.

440 B.C.: For the 85th Olympiad Polykleitus sculpts the Doryphorus [*Spear-bearer*], establishing the athletic kanon followed by later artists.

Unsung Boxers c.450 B.C.

The following boy boxers probably won their Olympik victories during or after the career of Diagoras: Gnathon [*Jawbone*] and Damoxenidas [?] of Maenalus; Lukinus [?] of Elis; Kritodamas [*Excellent-subduer*] and Alketus [?] of Kleitor; Thersilokhus [*?-platoon*] of Korkyra; Aristion [*Best-?*] of Epidauros.

**Figure 73.
Assistant Trainer at Work**
Attic kelix, 480 B.C.

This body work seems to be a simple sports massage given by one athlete to another to help warm up the muscles before a contest, or prior to training, or to rub out a knot during a break in the activity. The muscle being addressed seems to be the quadratus lumbarum, a lower back muscle that often knots up in boxers and is aggravated by the twisting motion of correctly throwing a rear hand power punch. A judge, trainer or gymnasiarch looks on.

The Gods of Boxing

Figure 74.
Athenian Boxers IV
From an Attic kelix

This is a superb example of classical high-handedness.

To the left two boxers apply hand straps.

The judge or trainer is confining the defensive boxer to the right with his rod and his extended foot. This could be an effective way to keep fighters in action if the official could rely on a wall or row of columns to his left. The fighter wrapping his hands also makes a convenient barrier.

The rightmost fighter is in the classic defensive posture. He is either attempting to measure the aggressor with his palm or spear him in the eyes with his fingers. His extended right appears to be a spent straight punch. The bent aspect of his left knee suggests that he has lunged with his lead hand and is not being entirely defensive. This fighter should step around to the left. With this in mind it seems probable that he is being coached by a trainer who is reminding him to step to his lead side against the left-hander's attack.

The fighter moving forward on the left is accelerating off of his rear foot. He may be applying a long trap [a controlling slap] to his opponents arm, or is lunging with a finger jab to the eyes. The rear left hand is being carried high to defend against a right-handed counter down the middle. If he successfully picks off the defender's right hand counter with his forearm or elbow then he will be in an excellent position to score with a lateral hammer-fist, possibly with a shift.

Both of these boxers are well-schooled combat athletes.

The other half of this piece, which is not reproduced here, depicts a pair of young wrestlers supervised by an official bearing a rod and staff. There are also boys, one practicing with jumping weights, one wrapping his hands, and another with a garment wrapped around his waist as he prepares the ground with a long-handled pick which has a narrow blade some two feet long.

The officials' staves all have a flat pummel, giving the appearance of a walking cane.

The Gods of Boxing

Figure 75-A.
Hand-Strapping
From the interior of an Attic kelix, 480 B.C.

The boy wrapping his right hand is passing the strap across the back of the hand and is keeping his fingers open, both aspects of modern hand wrapping. His technique differs from the common modern method in that the hand is held high over the right shoulder instead of being kept in front of the body. This would help to maintain the kind of tension that may be desirable with a leather wrap but not with cloth.

The Gods of Boxing

Figure 75-B
Sparring
From the exterior of the same Attic kelix pictured in 75-A

The sparring appears to be going on under the xystos [covered track] of a palaestra [wrestling school]. The fighter to the left has his left held high to block his opponent's jab and then counter with a hammer-fist to the bicep—which hurts like hell! He has his right chambered for the looping uppercut which appears to be meant for the other boxer's chin.

The rightmost boxer has missed with his jab and is fading back from his right knee [notice the bend] to avoid eating the opponent's oncoming uppercut. He is in the perfect position to throw a straight right to the heart or chin.

To the right of these fighters are two pankratiasts eye-gouging, fish-hooking and punching on the ground while being whipped by their trainer. This scene, and the savage nature of most of the boxing, makes one wonder if these trainers—wearing the garments that denote authority at naked athletic competitions and training sessions—were acting as judges in preliminary bouts to establish eligibility for drawing lots for an agon. It is well known that the ancients only wanted to see the best compete, and limited daylight did impose a time constraint. Perhaps these palaestra scenes that figure so prominently in Athenian art of this period not only demonstrate the character of high-handedness as a boxing style, but the nature of the selection process for the Panathenaic agons.

The Gods of Boxing

Figure 76.
Unskilled Athenian Boxers
From the exterior of the Attic kelix featured in Figure 75-A & B, 480 B.C.

To the right a fighter waiting his turn wraps his left hand as he looks on. The hand strap for his right is draped over the pillar against which he stands. From the looks of his build and poise he is probably the best of this trio. Behind him hangs a set of hand straps.

These two boxers have rigid extended guards and poor hand discipline. Those fingers and thumbs should not be spread out. By the calm demeanor of the judge/trainer this looks to simply be a sparring session—or maybe he's just given up on these two?

The fighter to the left has the superior position with his lead foot disrupting his opponent's base and his rear foot possibly stepping on the other's lead foot. He is trapping the opponent's left jab with an extended right—which would horrify most modern Chinese boxing teachers—and seems to be reaching out with his left to stop the other man's hammer-blow. If successful this would leave him in an excellent attitude to deliver a short right to the chin.

The flat-footed fighter on the right needs to step around to the left and jab, but is fading back off his right knee as he chambers a hammer-blow that he can't shift into.

To the left of the judge, and not depicted in this reproduction, is a heavy-armed-runner wearing shield and leg-guards and carrying his body armor in hand, perhaps preparing for a qualifying heat.

The Gods of Boxing

Figure 77.
Boxers Lining up For Inspection
From an Attic cup fragment by Makron, 480 B.C.

This is another example of combative Athenian tableware. One supposes that the ancient Athenian version of a "Tupperware party" was a meeting of fight afficianados, with more the character of a modern Superbowl party than a gathering of homemakers.

To the right is a pick for preparing the boxing ground.

Five young fighters with bundles of hand straps in their left hands, and right hand and forefinger raised in the attitude of submission, approach the judges and/or trainers.

The officials stand before a tripod and receive the boxers for inspection. The tripod may be the prize for the agon, or it may contain the school's body oil. As this piece is heavily damaged it is necessary to speculate. If this is a prize tripod, than the boys may be advancing to draw their lots, in which case one will draw a bye and sit out the first round. If this tripod contains the olive oil donated by the local athletic official, than the boys may be advancing to receive a ladle-full of oil to apply before training.

However, we must note that there is now substantial reason—other than our own modern notions of athletic development and fair play—for believing that practice and competition were fundamentally different in character during this period.

Figure 78.
Lapiths and Centaurs
From an Attic column-krater, c.465 B.C.

The central figure in this mythic battle is a fine welterweight demonstrating the posted power- jab which appears to have accounted for more Classical KOs than any other punch.

This vase depicts an episode from the mythic marriage feast of Perithous. The wrestler in the background is swinging the monster with a vicious neck crank, and the beast—who is still holding on to the table he was using as a weapon in this drunken brawl—is attempting to break his fall with his outstretched left rather than have his face hit the stone floor first.

The Gods of Boxing

Such scenes are common in Greek art, with the Lapiths representing the disciplined Greek athlete, and the Centaurs representing the barbaric horsemen of Southwest Asia, such as the Skythians.

Figure 79.
Polydeukes
From a marble statue by Pythagoras of Rhegion, c.450 B.C. [I am not qualified to date art. I would have dated this piece at 350 B.C. My source might be mistaken, so I offer the third paragraph below with some reservations.]

The Gods of Boxing

Polydeukes [*Very-sweet*], the mythic Greek version of Sugar Ray Robinson, is depicted throwing a body punch to the solar plexus with a straight vertical right fist, as he blocks a hammer-fist—that would have been thrown by the titanic brute Amykos—with his left forearm. This sequence would have been accomplished by blocking the downward hammerfist with a rising forearm block and instantly shifting the right leg forward as the hyper-pronated right fist held with elbow back at the collarbone was swung down by pulling the raised elbow into the body, thereby dropping the fist down into a vertical alignment and thrusting it forward with the shifting step.

Mechanically the lower body of this statue is depicted as having executed the very same maneuver used against James J. Corbett by Robert Fitzsimmons on March 17th 1897. [Fitzsimmons was the lightest man to ever win a modern heavyweight title.] The upper body mechanics of this sculpture are identical to those demonstrated by American heavyweight Joe Jeannette in a promotional photo with opponent Jim Stewart before their bout on April 28th, 1908.*

This sculpture shows the first signs of a change in hand-gear that would transform the sport within 130 years. The new aspect of this hand-strap is a longer wrap and a padded ring on the blocking point of the forearm, which was probably made of fleece [wool]. The physique of this sculpture of the god of boxing would, of course, represent the body type that was regarded as perfect for that sport at that time. We may guess that Theogenes of Thasos, the invincible boxer, or Diagoras of Rhodes, the most popular boxer, served as templates for Pythagoras, who undoubtedly viewed their statues at Olympia.

The stylistic and equipment differences between this depiction of a boxer and the vast majority of the boxers depicted in this period could stem from the fact that virtually all of the extant boxing art from this period is Athenian. This piece was fashioned by an Italian Greek. The traveling time separating ancient Athens and Region was far greater than that separating Ukrainian and Cuban boxers in the 21st Century. One must accept the fact that this survey of surviving evidence, must, by its very nature, fail to identify regional fighting styles, beyond Athens—which was not even regarded as much of a fight town. The fact is, that the fighters that we see depicted in that vast body of Athenian art, were almost always eaten alive in national competitions by the fighters from the islands, the cities of the Asian coast, and the Italian colonies.

*Joe Jeannette was a black American fighter who had a hard time finding white opponents. He fought the longest bout of the 20th Century on April 17th of 1909 in Paris against fellow shunned black contender Sam McVey. Jeannette hit the canvas 27 times, and got up to knock down McVey 11 times, winning the bout by KO in the 49th round! He fought exhibitions until age 66, having retired with 154 recorded bouts, with: 72 wins, 9 losses, 9 draws, 64 no-decisions, and 56 wins by KO. Most 21st Century boxing fans do not know his name. It is little wonder that the ancient Greeks, whose religious beliefs did not offer the hope of heaven that might have comforted Joe Jeannette, fought so hard for the right to have their name carved in stone.

Figure 80.
Sparing Head-gear
From a marble head of uncertain date

The head-gear depicted on this marble sculpture of a young boxer was probably reserved for use by boys, most of whom would not go on to compete as adult boxers, and wished to preserve their good looks, as beauty in ancient Greece was equated with inner goodness. The piece is identical to modern wrestling head gear and would only protect from "cauliflower ear", caused by an accumulation of ruptures, and could also prevent some cuts to the forehead. This sculpture was placed at this stage of our chronology because marble had just come into more general use, and because the slapping and trapping techniques of high-handedness would have encouraged its use among boys by this period in time.

Figure 81.
Boxer at Rest
From an Attic krater fragment by the Peleus Painter, c.445B.C.

This boxer is still wearing the light hand-straps that would remain common for the next 75 years. He appears to be looking on. Perhaps he has just finished wrapping and is sitting out a heat because he drew a bye. Such wraps would have to be re-wrapped between each bout, particularly in light of the open handed defensive tactics of the time.

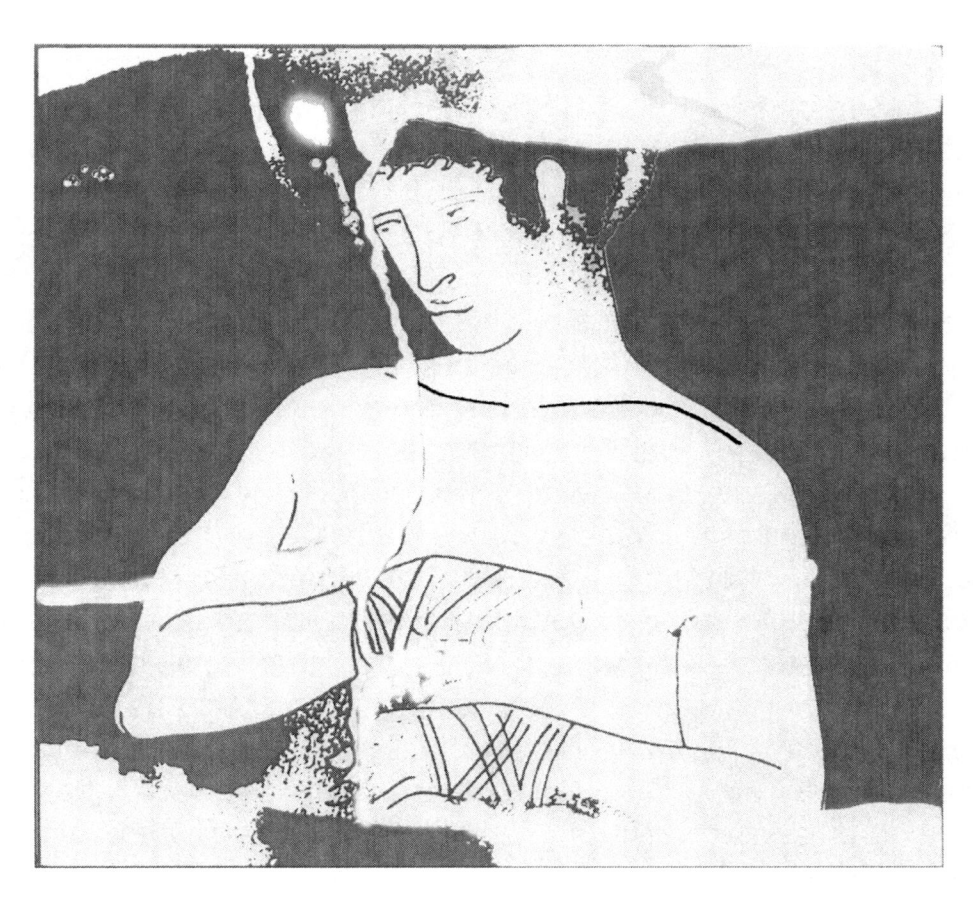

Boxing From 439 to 412 B.C.

"Whoever stands up to fight Eros against the hands of a boxer is not in his right mind."

-Sophokles, Trakhiniae

Eurydamas [*Broad-subduer*] of Cyrene, a Greek colony on the African coast south of Greece, was reputed to have won an Olympic crown in boxing by swallowing his teeth after eating his opponent's best punch. His opponent is said to have quit out of discouragement concerning his ability to hurt Eurydamas.

"There came the hard blows on to my face.
  For they had no steel in hand, nor we;
  But there were clenched fists raining blows..."

-Euripides, Iphigeneia in Taurika

c.439 B.C.: Upon the death of Theogenes the people of Thasos raise a statue in his honor. Afterwards an old enemy of Theogenes would come each night to beat the statue [presumably with a rod]. Eventually the statue fell and crushed the old man. The man's sons, according to the Athenian laws of Drako, charged the statue with homicide, and the Thasians duly convicted it and cast it out to sea. After a series of bad harvests the Thasians consulted the Delphic Oracle who blamed the forsaking of "your great Theogenes" for the ills that had befallen his homeland. The elders were at a loss as to how to recover the statue when fishermen brought it up in their nets by chance. The statue, with a circular marble offering box and an inscription specifying the standard offering [$5] and the use of collected funds [rediscovered in the 20th Century], was restored and the worship of Theogenes the healer was established. Theogenes was believed to have been fathered by the god Herakles who took possession of Theogenes' earthly father in order to conceive him. It is not known if this belief was current during his life or posthumous.

335 B.C. Dorieus [*Spear-lord*] of Rhodes, younger son of Diagoras, began competing as a boxer and pankratiast, but primarily as a pankratiast. With Eudicus the Athenian clown making fun of boxers and wrestlers perhaps Diagoras chose the pankration over boxing as a more fitting venue for his abilities.

The Gods of Boxing

431 B.C.: The Peloponnesian War breaks out. It is a nasty civil war the spreads like a cancer for an entire generation, and makes traveling to certain agons at certain times extremely dangerous.

429 B.C.: The Spartan siege of Athens and the horrific plague that breaks out drastically reduces the production of popular athletic art, such as tableware painted with boxing scenes.

"...but for heroic-combat,
   Victory with fist or with the hand, oxen were the prize..."
      -Euripides, *Alkestis*

424 B.C.: The eclipse of the sun, accompanied by the first recorded use of a flame-thrower, were two of the many events that marked this year as one of bad omens. At the 89th Olympiad Hellanikus [*Greek-victor*], son of Olympik boxer Alkaentus of Leaprus, beat the boys in boxing.

"By Zeus, if anyone had punched their jaws two or three times like Bupals, they would have no voice."
   -Aristophanes

421 B.C.: The "illusory" Peace of Nikias is proclaimed at Olympia, and the statue of Nike [*Winged-victory*] is created at Olympia by Paeonius. Aristophanes writes *Peace*.

420 B.C.: At the 90th Olympiad Theantus [?], younger son of Alkaentus of Lepreus wins the boy's boxing.

"A mighty roll and fists on the ears as a relish to go with it."
   -Aristophanes, *Eating Soldiers' Bread*

415 B.C.: The Athenian army winters at Naxos during the invasion of Sicily. Naxos, home of Tisander, the greatest Olympic boxer, disappears from the historical record after the doomed invasion.

"Those honoring the gods best in dance are best in war."
   -Sokrates

The Gods of Boxing

Figure 82.
Self-Massage
From the interior of an Attic kelix, 430 B.C.

These athletes are throwers of some kind; either pentathletes, boxers or pankratiasts. The man on the left appears to be checking his trapezius muscle for knots. Unless he's a real contortionist he'll need somebody else to actually rub out the muscle spasms. The man to the right is massaging the point where the forearm muscle attaches to the upper arm. This is a problem spot for boxers who get caught snapping out a jab that they reached too far for—and those Athenian boxers sure liked to pop that long jab!

The Gods of Boxing

Figure 83.
Holding on the Outside
From an Attic krater, 425 B.C.

      The two fighters on this vase are engaged in an outside clinch. Keep in mind that this is how Milo's last wrestling opponent avoided that fatal rib-cracking hug. They are both in an orthodox stance, and are not chambered for a hammerfist, indicating the evolution of more effective methods for delivering a straight right hand. The fighter advancing on the right appears to be grabbing and is being punished by the judge with his rod. Behind the judge hovers the mythic angel of winged victory, Nike, holding the crown of victory before her, perhaps as a reminder of the stakes one risks by fouling. In the foreground is a pedestal which either contains the sparring oil or the victory oil, depending on whether or not this is practice or competition—as always a difficult point to settle with Attic pottery of this period.

Boxing From 411 to 394 B.C.

411 B.C.: The revolt of Rhodes against Athens is led by Dorieus, who leads 18 ships into the Hellespont to link up with the Spartan fleet under Mindarus. The Rhodians were pursued by 20 Athenian ships. Dorieus had his men beach their ships, as the Athenians were the best sailors on open water, and fought from a beached position [going to the guard in essence], driving off the attackers. After both of these smaller fleets joined with the main battle fleets there was a large indecisive battle.

408 B.C.: Dorieus—now exiled by Rhodes under pressure from Athens who had condemned him to death—journeys to the 93rd Olympiad with his widowed sister Kallipateira [*Beautiful-?*] and her son Pisirhodes [*?-Rhodes*], and the adult son of his older sister Pherenike [*?-Victory*], Eukles [*Fair-honor*], and declares himself a citizen of Thurii in Italy. For the boy's boxing Kallipateira disguised herself as a trainer [Married-women being forbidden at the Olympics—just like modern boxing shows!] When Pisirhodes won his mother leaped over the fence [ring?] behind which the trainers were restrained and accidentally exposed herself. The Eleans threatened to toss her from the cliffs of Mount Typaion for breaking the taboo, but she claimed the right to attend based on the fame of her father, brothers and son, and was spared. However, future trainers would be required to attend in the nude. Eukles, apparently, seconded by Dorieus, won the men's boxing.

407 B.C.: Four Athenian ships under admiral Phanosthenes capture two renegade Rhodian ships under Dorieus. Despite the sentence of death declared by Athens, Phanosthenes lets Dorieus go without ransom on the pretext that he was now a citizen of Thurii, but in actuality, because he and his men greatly admired Dorieus and his family.

405 B.C.?: Euthymus, three-time Olympik victor of Lokri, having lived a distinguished and unnaturally long life, is said to have escaped death, by experiencing some type of ascension. Just as with Glaukos and Theogenes, Euthymus [*Grace-speaking*] was said to have been the son of a divine father. Although he was "called" the son of Astykles, he was said to be the son of the river Kaekinus, which divides his homeland of Lokri from the land of Region. The river was said to have magical properties that barred the grasshoppers of Region, which did not sing, from crossing into Lokri, which had normal musically inclined grasshopers. The reader should keep in mind that Greek myth vested rivers with masculine qualities, often at odds with mankind's atrocious behavior. The classical example from the Iliad was the rage of the river Skamander against Achilles for choking its water with the dead he had

slain. Euthymus was the most respected boxer in ancient history and the most selfless of famous men, and was later praised by the Hellenistic poet Menander [c.310 B.C.] who tended to be critical of prize-fighters.

404 B.C.: End of the Peloponnesian War. At the 94th Olympiad Kharmides [?] of Elis becomes one of the many victors in boy's boxing to have their likeness immortalized in the Altis in the late Classical period. Others includes Agiades [?] and Euaklidas [*Fair-?*] of Elis, Epikradius [?] of Mantineia, Tellon [*Complete*] of Oresthas, Skaeus [?] of Samos, Bykelus [?] of Sikyon, Dameretus [*Subduer-?*] of Messene, Xenodikus [*Honored-stranger-friend-?*] of Kos, Ageles [?] of Khios, and Butas [?] of Miletus.

401 B.C.: At the Nemean agon Kreugas [*Sacrificial-gut*] of Epidauros meets Damoxenos [*Subduing-honored-stranger-friends*] of Syrakuse in the final round of boxing when the sun began to set. The fighters agreed before witnesses to each allow the other in turn an open punch. Kreugas got the first punch, struck Damoxenos' head, and failed to knock him out. Damoxenos asked Kreugas to raise his left arm and speared him under the left ribs with his fingertips, which—due to the force of the blow and the sharpness of the nails—pierced Kreugas' abdomen. Damoxenos grabbed Kreugas' intestines and tore them out, killing him on the spot. Since it was obvious to the Argive judges that Damoxenos had practiced this cruel blow to perfection, and intentionally killed his opponent, they convicted him of the bogus charge of striking three blows [one for each of the spearing fingers, indicating the type of spear hand he used] instead of the agreed upon one blow, awarded Kreugas the crown posthumously, and raised a statue in his honor at Argos.

The names of these two fighters, tied together with their actions, constitute a small portion of a significant body of evidence that has led the author to conclude that most fighters who have had their names recorded, had adopted names related to their exploits and fame. I do not think we are remembering them by the names given to them in childhood

400 B.C.: Hippias of Elis compiles the Olympik register. Xenophon and the 10,000 hold an agon at Trapezius with a mountainside boxing ring. Some of the fighters complained that the Spartan who selected the site for the dug-up picked a hazardous location. On this expedition Boiskus, a noted boxer of Thessaly, proved a poor soldier, dropping his shield, complaining of fatigue, and looting enemy dead in defiance of orders.

399 B.C.: The death of Sokrates at Athens.

395 B.C.: Rhodes revolts against its new Spartan overlords while Dorieus is traveling near Sparta, and the Spartans capture and execute Dorieus in retaliation, although he was now a citizen of Thurii. Dorieus' name

[*Spear-lord*], and the fact that he commanded numerous warships, does suggest that he was famed and named for his military exploits. Many athletes valued their military notoriety above athletic achievements.

394 B.C.: There is an Eclipse of the sun.

Figure 84.
Kreugas and Damoxenos at Nemea, 401 B.C.
Artist's interpretation, based on the description by Pausanias

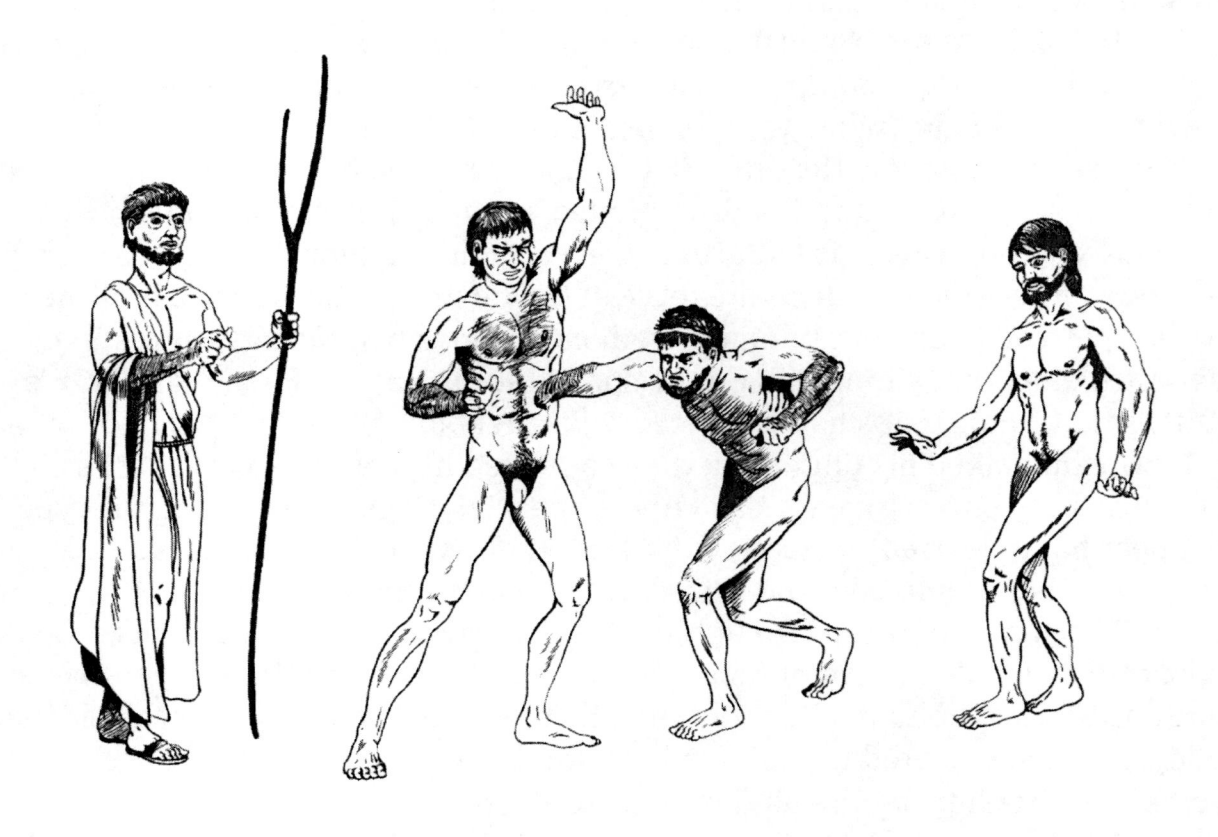

The Gods of Boxing

Boxing During the Tenure of Plato: 392 to 351 B.C.

"Athletes who are in a class of their own and win young, tend to grow slack and drop behind their rivals."
    -Sokrates, from Xenophon's *Memorabilia*

392 B.C.: At the 97th Olympiad the boy boxer Antipater [*Against-father*] of Miletus is offered a huge bribe by the agents of the tyrant Dionysius of Syrakuse to enter his name as a Syrakusian. Antipater and his father refused the bribe before going on to win in the boy's class with the fist. The men's fist was won by another Ionian, Phormiko [*Apollo's-lyre-player*] of Halikarnassos.

"So in the great games the unopposed victor is crowned the same as he who has fought for victory"
    -Xenophon, *Skripta Minora*

388 B.C.: The 98th Olympiad was rocked by scandal when Eupolus [*Fair-?*] of Thessaly was found to have bribed the other boxers in the men's class, including the previous champion Phormiko, Agenor [?] of Arkadia, and Pytanis [?] of Kyzikus—all disgraced as the crown was dedicated to Zeus, as were the fines, from which Zanes were raised. Those sleazy Thessalians just could not be trusted!

"...suppose the case of men who, having mastered boxing and pankration, did not compete, but attacked travelers; would you blame the instructors instead of putting to death those who used their skill for evil?"
    -Isokrates, *Antidosis*

372 B.C.: At the 102nd Olympiad Pisammon [?] of Athens wins with the fist. This is the probable date on which Neolaides [*New-?*] of Pheneus beat the boys with the fist.
368 B.C.: At the 103rd Olympiad Aristodamas [*Best-subduer*] wins with the fist.
366 B.C. Aristodamas wins with the fist at Delphi.
364 B.C.: At the 104th Olympiad Labax [*Much-announced*] of Lepreus, possibly a member of the second most successful boxing family in history, beat the boys with the fist.
362 B.C.: Aristodamas rterns to Delphi to win his second Pythiad.

The Gods of Boxing

360 B.C.: Chaereas [*Hand-?*] of Sikyon accompanies the much feared pankratiast Sostratus the "Finger-Breaker" to the 105th Olympiad, and defeats the boys in boxing.

356 B.C.: Chaereas returns to the 106th Olympiad and wins with the fist in the men's class.

351 B.C.: The landlord Pallados complains of a tenant—a "savage bruiser"—of his who is a brewer and former boxer, who threatened him with his fists when he came to his brewery to collect the rent.

Plato on Boxing: Excerpts from *Alkibiades II*, *Gorgias*, *Republic*, *Philebus* & *Laws*

"And the rules of boxing, I suppose, make a good boxer?"

"...if a fit man has become a good boxer at the wrestling school and strikes....kinsmen or friends we must not detest and banish for this reason our trainers......so too if a box practices his art wrongfully and injuriously......we should not censure or banish the instructor but rather the guilty man......And if the striker hits hard and fast the blow received must be of a like quality...Then the experience of the stricken is of the same quality as the action of the striker?....and perhaps someone will humiliate you by boxing your ears..."

"Do you think that one excellent boxer could easily fight two fat rich men who knew nothing of it? Would not such a fighter down a number of such opponents? Doubtless......it wouldn't be surprising if he did. Well, don't you think that the rich are better boxers than [they are] soldiers...? It will be easy, then, for our athletes in all likelihood to fight with double and triple their number."

"Well yes, Sokrates, it does look like pleasure has been given a knockout blow by your arguments..."

"...the endurance of pain so common among us Sparatans in our boxing bouts and....foraging raids.... Surely if we were boxers, for days before the actual agon we would be learning how to fight and working ourselves hard...A man who has practiced pankration or boxing or is an excellent wrestler does not find himself unable to fight with his left [The speaker goes on to denounce boxing and ground-fighting tricks as less useful in war than ordinary stand-up wrestling.]...for the element of boxing in the pankration we shall substitute [combat with missile weapons]...If a man is struck by another his age, or a senior but childless man by a junior, whether the parties are both old or both young, he shall defend himself with the weapons nature has given him, his unarmed naked fists." [A denouncement of fights between young and old follows.]

**Figure 85.
The Boxing Effigy**
Artist's conception, based on the training aid mentioned by Plato

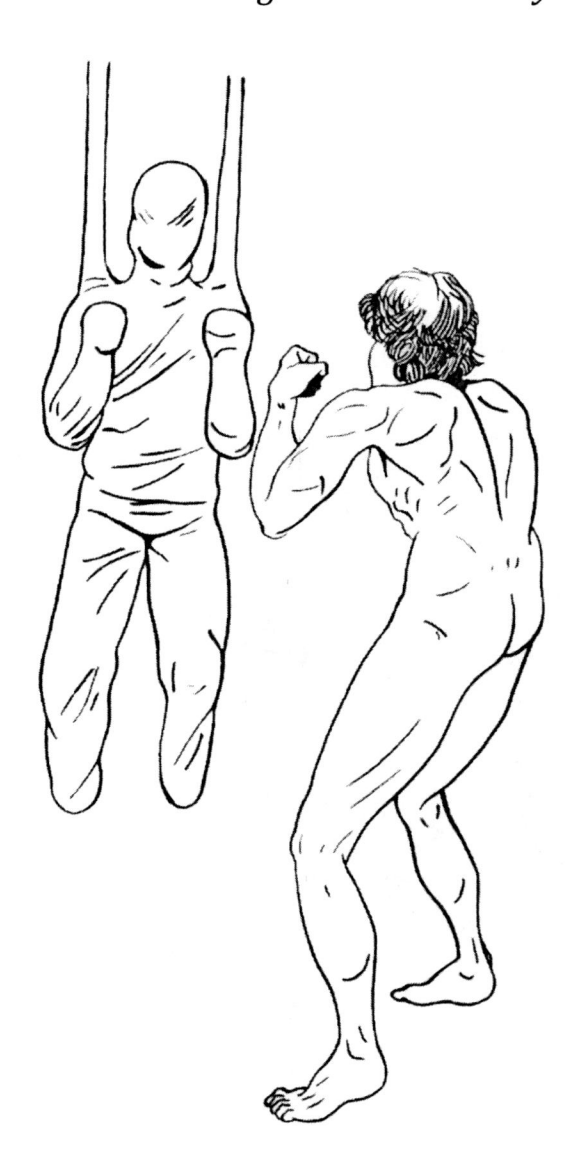

"...instead of hand-straps, we should use round gloves so that we may practice our punches and blocks all out. And if we lacked sparring partners, the ridicule of fools would not dissuade us from hanging up a lifeless image and practicing on it... It is only by frequent practice with the round gloves that a proper knowledge of blocking and punching can be acquired."
 -Plato, *Kleinias and the Athenian*

This type of anatomical punching target became popular in the 1990s, just as MMA came into its own. It might interest the reader that by the time of Plato, the pankration had achieved a status equal to or surpassing that of boxing. It may be that the increasing number of fighters who practiced boxing with an eye on its applications in the pankration, caused a greater interest in anatomically correct punching bags.

Figure 86.
Blood-thirsty Cherubs
From a Roman marble sarcophagus, probably 4th Century

Unlike the earlier depictions of boxing weights from Roman and Ilyrrian sources, these weights are grasped with heavy gauntlets, indicating boxing with these little clubs or training weights as one of a number of converging

The Gods of Boxing

trends in hand-gear that would result in the gladiatorial gauntlet of late antiquity.

The defeated cherub has signaled submission by the raising of his right hand, while in the reclining position of a dying gladiator. The victorious little fiend with his foot tastelessly placed on the leg of the defeated cherub and his hand uncharacteristically [for an ancient victor] raised in celebration accepts the palm of victory from the official.

One would suspect this to be a comic by a Roman artist making fun of Greek combat, except for the uncomfortable fact that this graced the panel of a rich man's sacred resting place—and the Romans took their ancestors seriously. The occupant must have been a boxing fan.

Figure 87.
Youths Boxing
From a panAthenaic amphora, c.350 B.C.

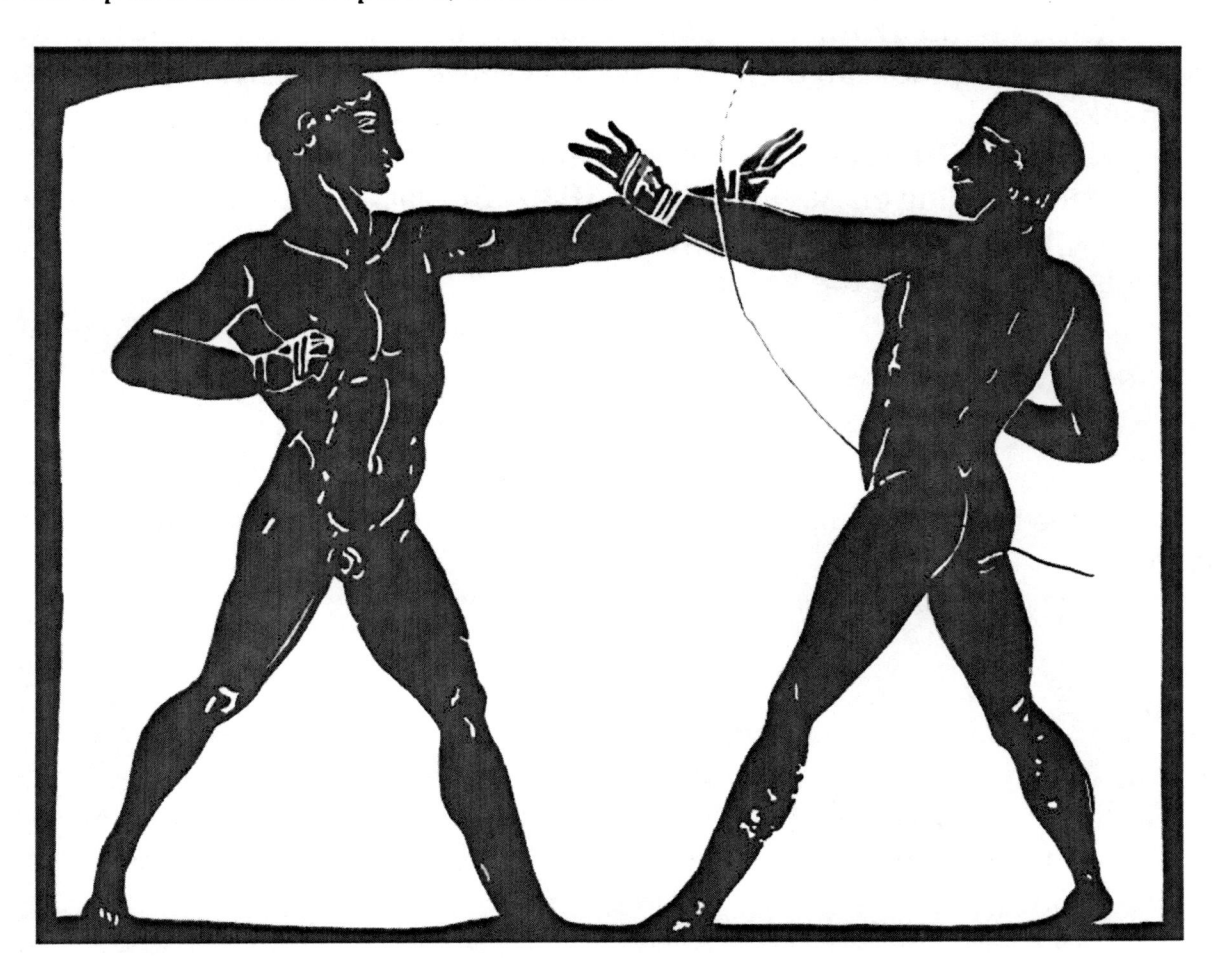

The evolution of Greek boxing is nearly complete at the period of this piece, depicting fighters pawing with an extended left guard at long range while measuring one another for a straight right. It appears that the extended guard was developed as a counter to the rear hand hammer-fist and long range uppercut, which have now been abandoned for the straight right. The right hand serves the same function here as it would in the English bare-knuckle tradition: to protect the body, and to attack the body and face. The extended lead can—and surely was—folded over with the fist being pointed down to shield the body with the hanging forearm and the face with the raised elbow.

The posture depicted would only be used by both combatants at the start of a bout and at the point of restoring outer range after an exchange. Someone would soon get the worst of this game and fold the arm over or pull the elbow back in order to advance, guard or counter. Greek boxers certainly didn't abandon the power jab, which had been the foundation of their arsenal before and after the period of this illustration.

Keep in mind that the use of hand-straps in pankration competition was known, if not common. So it may be that this represents the kickboxing phase of a pankration bout. Also remember that the hammer-fist never completely disappeared from the arsenal of the ancient fighter and was only eradicated from modern boxing on August 27th of 1889 after Jack Dempsey was knocked out by a spinning hammer-fist thrown by George LaBlanche, who was over-the-weight, and a little too French to boot....

Boxing during the Tenure of Aristotle: 351 to 325 B.C.

"...those who practice boxing and the like ruin their minds as well as their bodies..."
        -Demosthenes, *The Erotic Essay*

c.350 B.C.: The Pantheniac agon pays out the following awards for boxing: Boys' 1st place = 30 jugs of olive oil [$12,00], boys' 2nd place = 6 jugs [$2,500]; youths' 1st place = 50 jugs [$20,000], youths' 2nd place = 10 jugs [$4,000]; men's 1st place = 60 jugs [$24,000], men's 2nd place = 10 jugs [$4,000].

The Gods of Boxing

344 B.C.: At the 109th Olympiad Khoerilus [?] of Elis defeats the boys with the fist.

340 B.C.: At the 110th Olympiad Theotimus [*God-?*] of Elis won the crown for the boy's boxing.

"But all, or at least many, know what Euthynus [*Fair-?*], the renowned wrestler, a youth, did to Sophilus [*Wisdom-fond*] the infamous fist-all-power-fighter. He was dark and brawny. Surely some of you know of the man I speak. They met in Samos at a gathering—a private party—and because he imagined [that Sophilus] was insulting him, took revenge and actually killed him."
    -Demosthenes, *Against Meidias*

"...like barbarians who box, who, not knowing how to slip a punch, simply follow it and get hit."
    -Demosthenes, *2nd Phillipik*

339 B.C.: Satyrus [*Goat-man*] of Elis beats the men with the fist at Nemea. Satyrus, son of a prominent Elean clan, shuns the Isthmian agons, due to the Curse of Moline or Lysippe.

338 B.C.: Phillip of Makedon defeats the Greeks led by Demonsthenes at the battle of Khaeronei. Satyrus is victorious with the fist at the 61st Pythiad.

"Rods [punishments] and toils unmeasured."
    -Axiokhos on training

337 B.C. Satyrus wins at Nemea.

336 B.C.: At the 111th Olympiad Aristotle updates the Olympic register, Alexander—having succeeded his slain father—sets up ivory statues of himself and his family next to the statue of Theogenes in the Altis. Satyrus dominates the boxers.

335 B.C. Satyrus wins at nemea.

334 B.C.: Alexander [*Protector-of-men*] the Great of Makedon begins his ultimately genocidal and suicidal invasion-quest of the vast Persian Empire. He brings numerous Greek athletes, and his men cart along loads of wrestling dust, in order that he might dedicate proper agons to his patron gods Zeus and Herakles in celebration of his triumphs. Satyrus wins with the fist at the 62nd Pythiad.

333 B.C. Satyrus wins at Nemea.

332 B.C. Satyrus wins his second Olympic boxing victory.

331 B.C. Satyrus wins boxing again at Nemea

330 B.C. A bronze statue of Satyrus, commemorating his career is raised in the Altis at Olympia. It will be recovered some 2,300 years later.

328 B.C.: Alexander the Great punches his trumpeter while drunk in Sogdia.

327 B.C.: Alexander's army encounters boxers in northwest India. Aristibolus wrote "Among some tribes, penniless virgins were married off as the prizes for boxing bouts." This pretty much demolishes the theory that the martial arts of China and Japan were derived from Indian martial arts which had been imparted to the Indians by the superior Greeks. Indian boxing and wrestling probably grew out of the same Indo-European tradition that saw the rise of these arts in Iraq, Crete, Egypt and Greece.

Aristotle on Boxing: Excerpts from his Nikomakhaen Ethics

Aristotle was fascinated by the fact that more was known about the athletic sciences than about the science of navigation. Overall he seemed to understand boxing better than most thinkers of the day, and is the only source that sites the existence of a boxer of the day named Anthropos [*Manly-man*]. The *Nikomakhaen Ethics* were named after his son to a slave-woman, Nikomakhus [*Victorious-fighter*.]

"...nor does the boxing coach impose the same way of fighting on everyone."

"The end and object of courage is pleasant, but it is obscured by the surrounding circumstances: which is also the case with the naked arts; to the boxers the end is pleasant with a view to their actions—I mean the crown and the honors; but the blows they receive are painful and irritating to the flesh and blood, and so is all the labor they have to undertake, and as these drawbacks are many, and the objective seeming distant appears to have no pleasantness in it."

Figure 88.
Pre-fight Instructions
From a PanAthenaic amphora, 340-39 B.C.

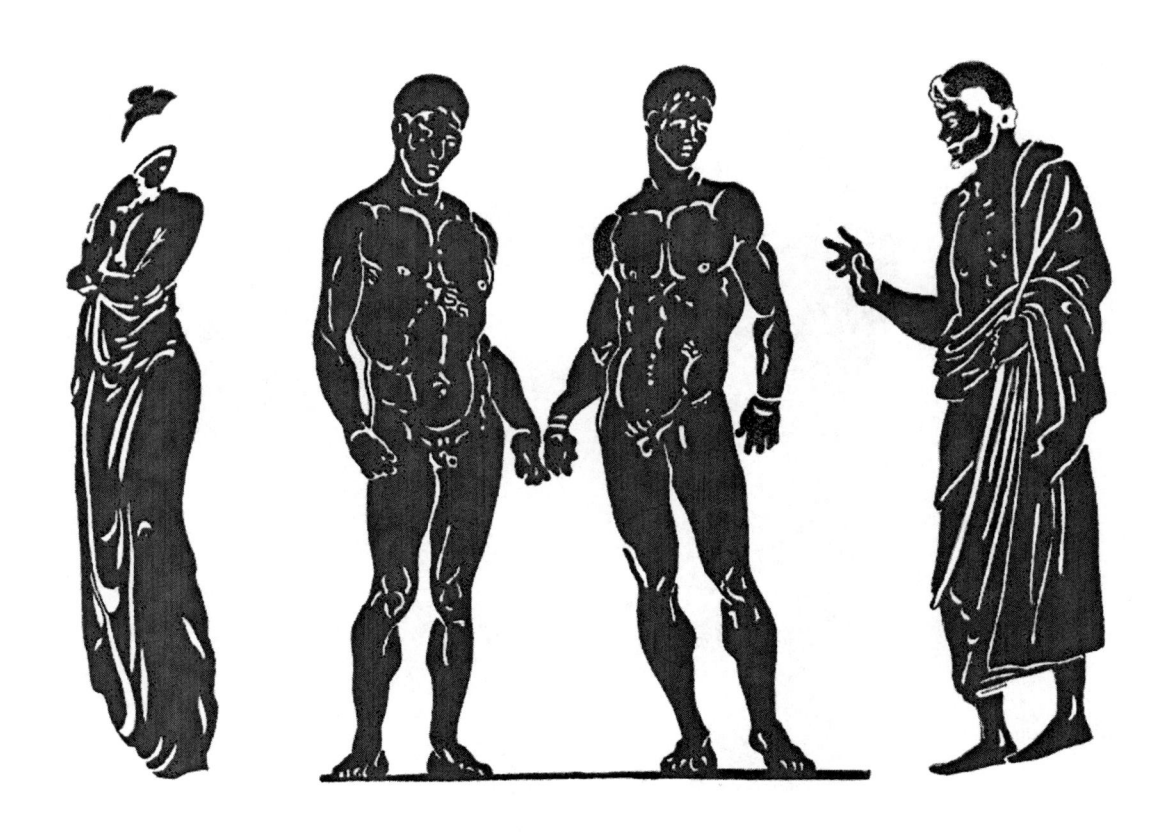

The judge instructs the fighters, who have their heads slightly downcast in the attitude of respect. The judge is taller than the fighters and has an atrophied chest, obviously a former athlete of great stature. The fighters look like cruiserweights and are obviously under six feet in height. Their hands are wrapped in light thongs, this being perhaps the last Athenian occasion for their use among the men. There does remain the possibility that these are pankratiasts using light hand-straps.

These competitors might be assigned to the 18-20 year-old category, or are younger entrants in the 21+ men's class. The divine personification of Olympia looks on with demure interest, indicating that victory in this local Athenian agon may lead to competition at the 111th Olympiad—some fresh-meat for Satyrus!

The Gods of Boxing

Figure 89.
Heavyweights with State-of-the-art Hand-gear
From a PanAthenaic amphora, 336 B.C. [See Figure 90 for more detail.]

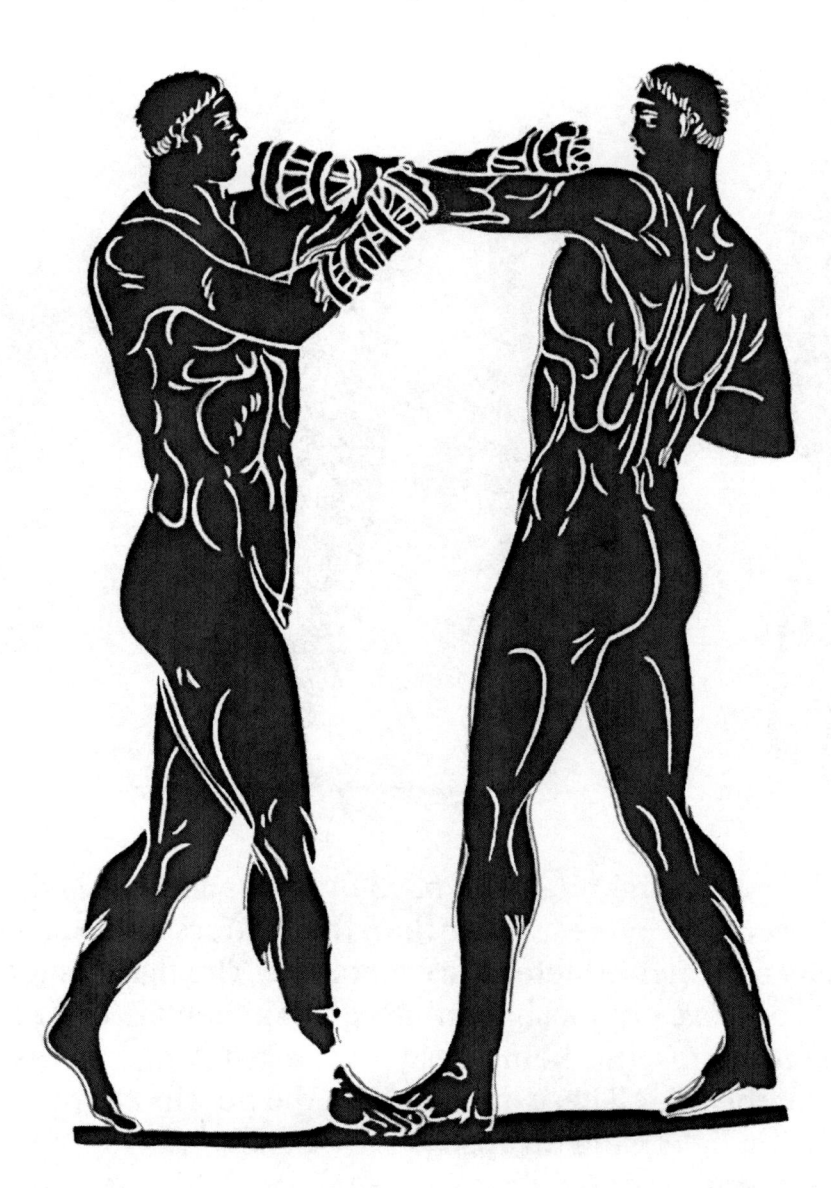

    This beautiful work was given as a boxing prize at the PanAthenic agon. The palm of victory to the back of the rightward fighter is held by the goddess Athena [not depicted in this reproduction].
    Overall this piece demonstrates a fuller exploration of the boxing applications of the postures depicted in Figure 87. The fighters are more muscular but not proportionately different than the statue of Polydeukes by

The Gods of Boxing

Pythagoras, and the hand-gear is an upgrade of the composite gear worn by that statue.

The hand-gear worn by these fighters consists of a fleece forearm sleeve [for padding], overwrapped by two sets of handstraps. Hand-gear of this type is a tremendous pain-in-the-ass to apply, especially when you must fit it yourself!

These are definitely heavyweights. It may also be of interest that these fighters [The author believes these figures to represent actual competitors from the previous agon, immortalized on the prizes for the next generation.] were probably among those who the pankratiast Dioxippos sparred with in preparation for his Olympic victory in 336, and that they most certainly fell victim to Satyrus of Elis or to someone who he eventually defeated if they entered to box at Olympia on that year.

This is a battle between a left handed fighter on the left and a righty on the right. The fighter on the left appears to be depicted in the moment leading up to victory as he steps to the outside of his opponent's lead foot, parries the single lift jab with his right, and launches a straight left. Although his opponent appears to be successfully fading from the straight left this will leave him back on his heels and unable to use his right hand, as the aggressor has stepped to the outside.

Expect the fighter on the left to exploit this near miss by pulling back his left, pivoting and jabbing with his lead right over the opponent's shoulder, which will probably only graze the head, but will set him up to throw the left straight down the middle. Although both fighters are in a good position to work the body they seem to be, like most modern heavyweights, head-hunters.

It appears to have taken the ancient Greeks 400 [750 to 350 B.C.] years to evolve a form of boxing similar to modern gloved boxing. It took modern boxing 200 years to evolve from its infancy in 1719 to its heyday in the 1920s and 1930s. There are deep questions concerning origins that we cannot answer definitely, and one cannot trust too much to the stream of extant art work. Remember, that the bout described by Homer in the Iliad more closely resembles the action depicted in this piece some 400 years later than it does bouts depicted in art 200 or 300 years after his writing. And this is propitious, because the nature of the source material for our study begins to change radically after the appearance of this particular jug.

Figure 90.
Tweaking the New Gear
From a panAthenaic amphora, 336 B.C. [a detail from Figure 89.]

This detail from the source for Figure 89. is a reminder, not only of the difficulty of applying this type of sophisticated hand-gear, but the fact that the south paw who apparently won the fight depicted above, had yet to fight this bruiser, who doesn't appear the least bit worried...

The Gods of Boxing

Figure 91.
Satyrus of Elis
From a bronze head at Olympia, 330 B.C.

Satyrus of Elis was the son of a powerful clan, yet sacrificed himself to the cruelest sport available. His face shows moderate trauma to the nose, at least three heeled cuts on the left forehead, and scar tissue around the left eye, indicating that he was a right-handed fighter. His thick beard and hair would have offered some protection, padding blows with a hard fist and deflecting the slashing edges of leather hand-straps.*

The Gods of Boxing

*Author's note: My rather light beard has provided some cushion against grazing punches in bare-knuckle and small-glove bouts. However, I still sustained two chin cuts. One amateur fighter I took to a bout with a stylish go-tee was made to shave it before fighting. *USABoxing* bans beards because of the danger of getting a loose course hair ground into a fighter's eye during a clinch. Those rare beards among modern pros are sometimes a point of contention, with opponent's charging that the beard might cushion a blow. Overall modern coaches don't like bald heads because they get cut easier, and don't like long hair because a head with long hair makes a greater visual impact on the judges when it gets hit, and because old white guys don't like stuffing a guy's pony tail under his headgear in the gym. In one small-glove bout my pony-tail came undone and became matted to my face from the sticky blood that spewed from my nose. Looking for my tormentor through strands of dark gooey hair definitely placed me at a disadvantage.

Analysis of Classical Boxing Techniques in Literature & Art: 520-336 B.C.

"That's it! You're boxing like an American now!"
  -Frank Gilbert, January 28, 2005

Strike Type of 88 Strikes

Fist	Digit	Palm	Dumbbell
77%	3%	13%	7%

Amplification of 88 Strikes

None [arm]	Linear [straight]	Rotational [hook]	Angular [uppercut]	Gravitational [hammer]
7%	62%	4%	15%	12%

Defenses Against 88 strikes

Head/Body Movement	Active Hand	Passive Hand	None
21%	33%	18%	28%

The Gods of Boxing

A Stylistic Summary of Classical Boxing

First let us review the findings of the study above in contrast to the study of archaic Greek boxing.

1. The Classical boxer became more reliant on the fist as a weapon and less likely to jab with the fingers or thumb. This is a conservative trend which favored a more reliable weapon which could be honed in sparring. The increase in palm use can be explained by the lightening of the hand gear. However, the decrease in the use of punching clubs probably reflects a trend toward unarmed ritual combat in Italy and Illyria as opposed to dueling, and has little bearing on the mainstream of Greek boxing.

2. The Classical boxer is more of a knockout puncher than his archaic predecessor. He is 650% more likely to put weight into his punches; 50% more likely to throw a straight right; no more likely to throw a hook—which is a sign that the hand-gear in use still provided minimal hand protection; was 250% more likely to throw an upper-cut—the most difficult punch to land; and was 300% more likely to throw a hammer-fist than were earlier fighters. Overall the strike amplification of the Greek boxer progressed from the archaic period from something that resembled the habits of a modern karate fighter to a set of habits reminiscent of the methods of the American Prize Ring c.1885, when the use of skin-tight gloves encouraged some particularly brutal tactics.

3. The Classical boxer was just as likely as the archaic fighter to simply eat a punch. However he was 60% more likely to slip or lean away from a punch; and 60% less likely to use a passive guard.

Overall the Classical Greek boxer was more of an action fighter than his grandfather, and was destined to win or lose by KO, rather than be forced to submit due to exhaustion, in most of his fights.

The Cultural Context of Boxing in Classical Hellas

Although wrestling in Classical Greece remained essentially a preparation for war, boxing became less so. Though boxing still had its timeless military use as a tool for the psychological conditioning of the foot soldier, it does not appear to have gained favor as a tool for the mental conditioning of leaders and bonding them to their men—this later being a key military use of boxing in the British military of the 18th and 19th Centuries.

In Classical Greece boxing became a central facet of the sacred otherworldly reality that leant meaning and stability to the spiritual lives of a culture that was suffering profound scientific shock and war-weariness, and looked to the mythic days of their ancestors for a world no less violent, but more whole and understanding. To the extent that athletics prepared leaders for war they would come from the ranks of the pentathletes and pankratiasts, but increasingly from the brutalized ranks of the professional soldiery. If anything military remained to be said for boxing besides coaching the young militia man in the virtue of facing the enemy, it was as a simple reminder that there had once been a day when war was a man-to-man duel, when most men bore witness to the killing rather than doing the killing, as opposed to joining in the ever-intensifying mass-slaughter of the battle-fields that dotted the landscape with increasing size and regularity as the time of Alexander and his successors neared.

Chapter 12
The Fate of Ancient Boxing

"What honor have you earned having prevailed over a weaker man? You might be tolerated if you had, by skill, overcome a stronger man."
   -Aesop

In the ancient world boxing was regarded as the consummate skill; the purest sport; an activity that did not have to serve a greater purpose. Apollo was the god of boxing, but first and foremost, he was the god of excellence; Arete, the excellence of the warrior, the cultivated man. To be a boxer was to be a person of quality, a man of moral and spiritual significance. The fist-fight was a moral struggle with oneself, the event, and the opponent.

Boxing as an art would mutate and survive, evolving for many centuries to remain relevant. And it would remain relevant, so long as men saw themselves as civilized members of city-based societies who shared a universal culture.

Boxing Before, During and After Alexander

"In the third fight he [Arturo "Thunder" Gatti] hit me and my brain shifted in my head and hit the back of my skull. Screwed up my peripheral vision. They [the surgeons] had to go in and even me off. Intense...Me and Arturo? Best of friends. I'll be in his corner for his next fight. It's weird how that happens."
   -"Irish" Mickey Ward, from an interview published in the *2005 Everlast Boxing Catalog*

Throughout this study we have explored the many ways in which various forms of ancient boxing differed from their modern counterparts. Western boxing traditions developed in association with particular weapon systems [the chariot, punching shield and stabbing sword*] and sacrificial rites. Long after the weapon arts that spawned boxing faded into obsolescence boxing continued to thrive as a martial art and spectacle. The spread, preservation, and resurrection of boxing has always depended, at least

The Gods of Boxing

in part, on its military usefulness as a method for the psychological conditioning of the individual soldier, as well as its use as a peer-bonding tool among members of the officer class, from Troy to West Point**.

Ultimately boxing is a martial ritual that serves the visceral, social, ethical and spiritual needs of the warrior, rather than addressing the specific technical issues of contemporary weapon-craft and military operations. As so brutally and matter-of-factly summed up by Mickey Ward, the act of boxing for the prize of victory serves the dual purpose of setting the boxer apart from the mass of ordinary people, while at the same time joining him with his opponent. The officer class descended from the staff of Alexander became an alien minority ruling over massive slave-societies. The nature of their cultural cohesion may be summed up in the phrase "boys from the gym" that they used to describe themselves. There is no greater indication of the singular metaphoric importance of boxing than this quaint, almost British-sounding, phrase.***

The forces that drove the metamorphosis of boxing in the time of Alexander and his successors where three, and each had its own profound influence on the conduct and context of Greek boxing:

1. At the fore was an increasingly predatory military matrix [Alexander himself presided over at least a dozen genocides] that demanded a more lethal war metaphor, in the form of the hardened leather boxing gauntlet, which had its origins among hand-strap boxers who allowed the striking portions of their soft wraps to stiffen and grow "sharp" with repeated use and intentional neglect.

2. Due to the military success of Greek arms the pool of contestants at sacral venues swelled and required a quicker resolution of bouts, which was nicely served by the more damaging boxing gauntlet.

3. As boxing became a less important aspect of preparation for military service, it came to be practiced almost exclusively by the officer and slave classes as a martial rite or entertainment; observed by an increasingly alienated audience with little or no appreciation for the technical aspects of the art, encouraging a dramatic and sadistic view of the art, which served the needs of poets and dictators alike.

As the brutally rustic life of the Homeric heroes was submerged beneath the dehumanizing realities of mass-warfare and plantation-slavery, boxing survived as an expression of the heroic ethic in an imperial age; an art of lonely toil embraced as a metaphor for masculine virtue by isolated military elites and as a sadistic spectacle by alienated commoners. As in modern times, the momentum of alienation brought the boxer to that cruel apex where one short step separated the riches of victory from the poverty of defeat.

*Plutarch's tale of the origins of boxing among the Spartans being related to their habit of conditioning themselves for fighting without helmets could be related to the legend of Polydeukes' boxing prowess, as Polydeukes was reputed to have been a Spartan ancestor, and a brother of Helen of Troy.

**Leduff, Charlie. *Only in America: Fight Club*, The Discovery Times Channel, September 2nd, 2005

This excellent series of experiential documentaries focuses on masculine subcultures. The Fight Club episode examines the day-to-day life of the East Bay Rats Motorcycle Club, the members of which use tough-man style boxing as a bonding ritual.

***Edgarton, Robert B. *Like Lions They Fought: The Zulu War and the Last Black Empire in South Africa*, Ballantine Books, NY, 1988, page 61.

Edgarton carefully examines the subculture of the Victorian British officer class, of which boxing was an integral facet, providing peer-bonding between officers and enlisted men. In an age when officers and men were physically and mentally so different as to appear like two barely-related subspecies of the human race, boxing provided the only level social interaction between these two extreme social classes.

The Gods of Boxing

Figure 111.
Apollo Jabbing the Centaur
From a relief from the piedemont of the Temple of Zeus at Olympia

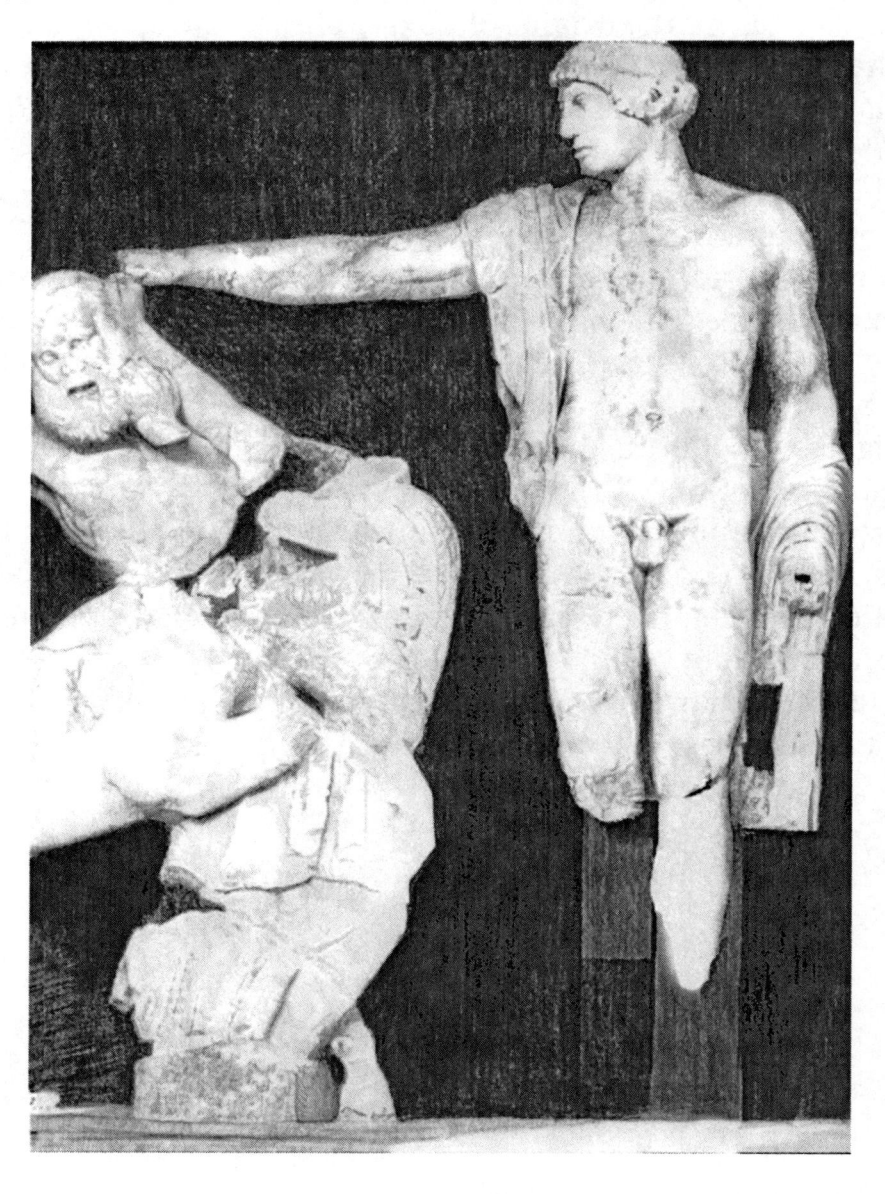

It is most telling that the only examples of boxing art from Classical Greece that demonstrate the technically optimal modern-style pronated and hyper-pronated jabs depict two lapiths [Figures 78 and 110] and the god of boxing, Apollo, striking centaurs. It might also be added that these very centaurs are depicted using effective combatives of their own: swinging a table; choking and kneeing; and covering and rolling with the punch, as depicted in this illustration.

168

Of particular interest, is the fact that Apollo, god of the sun, plagues, archery, charioteers, boxing, and the civilized arts, is depicted scientifically punching out a centaur; a race of man-horses supposedly fathered by his son Kentaurus, who had the bad-taste to mate with wild mares. Mating with a mare was an early and obscure Indo-European kingship ritual associated with horse-sacrifice, which has been demonstrably linked to the culture of the chariot-warrior, as has boxing. In fact, bestiality with horses was not taboo among the Hittites, who punished men who mated with other domestic animals. Where this tangled spiral of cultural associations ultimately points is a mystery beyond the comprehension of this author. However, the author and readers of this study have been given a great opportunity for wonder and conjecture by the ancient artist who sculpted this freeze on the temple of the Thunder Chief over 2,400 years ago.

Epilogue:
The Life of Boxing to A.D. 551

All entries are known facts. Theories are in brackets.

Dates B.C.
1800: Boxing in Mesopotamia
1600: Boxing in Crete
1500: Boxing on Thera
1350: Boxing in Egypt
1100: Boxing on Cyprus
1000: Boxing in Armenia
 884: Olympic treaty of Iphitis [boxing is a possible event]
 776: Olympic treaty of Lykurgus [boxing is a probable event]
 720: The Iliad of Homer describes a boxing match
 688: Onomastus of Smyrna is the first recorded victor in Olympic boxing
 616: Phylytas of Sibaris is the first recorded victor in boy's Olympic boxing
 588: Pythagoras of Samos defeats larger boxers at Olympia with superior skills
 586: 1st Isthmian agon
 582: 1st Pythian *agon*
 573: 1st Nemean Agon
 572: Olympis become panHellenik [open to all Greeks]
 566: 1st PanAthenean agon
 556: Damagetus becomes the last Spartan to win boxing at Olympia
 544: The statue of Praxidamas of Aegina is erected at Olympia for boxing
 528: Tisander of Naxos becomes the first and only boxer to win 4 Olympic crowns
 520: Glaukos of Karystos win's Olympic boy's boxing with a hammer-fist punch
 500: Boxing in Italy
 496: Kleomedes versus Ikkos at 71st Olympiad
 480: Theogenes versus Euthymus at 75th Olympiad
 448: Diagoras of Rhodes retires from boxing as his sons are crowned at Olympia
 411: Timokreon of Rhodes boxes at the court of the Persian king
 408: The grandsons of Diagoras win boy's and men's boxing at Olympia

The Gods of Boxing

401: Kreugas versus Damoxenos at Nemea
388: Boxers Eupolus and Phormiko caught in bribery scandal at Olympia
330: The likeness of Olympic boxer Satyrus of Elis is sculpted in bronze
270: The *Dioskuri* of Theokritus describes gauntlet boxing
258: A raised boxing platform is built at Delphi for the Pythian agons.
250: The *Aurgonautika* of Apollonius describes gauntlet boxing
218: Paeanius of Elis wins boy's and men's boxing at Pythia
214: Kleitomakhos of Thebes sweeps the three combats at the Isthmian agon
212: Kleitomakhos versus Aristonikus at the 142nd Olympiad
186: Boxing at Rome
160: The first athletic synod [fighters' union] is organized at Sardis
100: Black African boxers are depicted in art
 48: Atyanas of Adramyttium wins boxing at the 182nd Olympiad
 41: The Sardis synod is sanctioned by the Roman Republic
 18: The *Aeneid* of Virgil describes gauntlet boxing
 12: A boy boxer is bribed by his opponent's father at the 192nd Olympiad

Dates A.D.
 38: The Roman Emperor Caligula employs a troupe of African boxers
 49: Melenkomas "The Elder" of Karia wins boxing at the 207th Olympiad
 61: The Roman Emperor Nero forces senators to box at spectacles
 62: Saint Paul discusses boxing in his *Letters*
 80: Melenkomas "The Younger" versus Iotrakles at Rome
 82: *The Argonautica* of Flaccus describes gauntlet boxing
 90: *The Thebaid* of Statius describes gauntlet boxing
 92: The town of Tauromenium holds 81 agons [with boxing tournaments]
 93: Apollonius versus Herakleides at the 218th Olympiad-turned-comedy
 99: The Sardis synod is sanctioned by the Emperor Trajan and moved to Rome
117: Tullius of Apamea becomes the only double *periodinikes* in boxing
125: Didas versus Garapammon at the 226th Olympiad—both fined for bribery
129: The *Synod of Sacred Victors* and *Synod of Athletes* merge at Rome under the
      Imperial *Synod of the Herkulanei* [formerly of Sardis]
168: Damostratus of Sardis is undefeated in boxing
177: Damostratus appointed head of athletics for the Roman Empire
194: The boxer Herminos is admitted to the Naples synod for 100 denarii

200: Agothos Daimon wins boxing at Nemea
201: Agothos Daimon dies boxing at the 245th Olympiad
211: Gladiatorial boxing at Rome
218: Banquet boxing under Emperor Elagabalus
229: Gerenius dies at his victory feast after having won boxing or pankration at the
     252nd Olympiad
252: CoEmperor Gallus enjoys gladiatorial boxing at Antioch
253: Conquering Emperor Gallienus has male and female boxers fight with ancient soft
     handstraps at his triumph at Rome
284: Victorious prize-fighters exempted from public service by Emperor Diocletian
357: Emperor Constantius II is a big boxing fan
385: Prince Varzadates of Persia [later King of Armenia] wins boxing at the 291st
     Olympiad
393: The last sanctioned Olympic agon—no victors recorded
400: *The Fall of Troy* of Quintus of Smyrna describes gauntlet boxing
408: Athletic sanctuaries in Greece destroyed by Imperial decree
450: The *Dionisika* of Nonnos describes gauntlet boxing
500: 14 athletes sign a victory plaque at Olympia
522: Olympia damaged by earthquake
529: Code of Justinian repeals the privileges of athletes
551: Olympia ruined by earthquake

Appendix
A Discussion of the Literary Sources

"Education is not the filling of a pail, but the lighting of a fire."
  -William Butler Yeats

The Three Layers of Historical Knowledge

The source material utilized in researching this work was subdivided early in the process according to the following scheme:
1. Tertiary, or information two or more steps removed from the ancient source
2. Secondary, or information one step removed from the ancient source
3. Primary, or preserved ancient sources

The study of all three of these categories is essential to the researcher, and each presents various barriers capable of frustrating efforts at critical examination. Now, let us proceed with caution back through the ages as we examine some of the most prominent sources of each type.

Tertiary Sources

In general sources two or more steps removed from the subject are of minor importance and serve primarily to educate the author as to the opinions held by modern authors who have done little or no research into the subject. It is a minefield of ill-conceived notions and factual errors interspersed with islands of profound insight.

Websites, Magazines & Television Documentaries: Most of these contain numerous key-punch or production errors and are so poorly researched and sourced that they are of little or no value to the reader as he begins his search. However, once enough primary research has been done to enable the researcher to winnow away the multitude of errors, one may glean useful tidbits from the websites and valuable opinions from the more passionate academics interviewed on the documentaries. The pace at which videos,

The Gods of Boxing

websites, and magazines are produced discourages the type of editing that tends to keep authors of books in check.

Boxing and martial arts Books: Most "factual" discussions on ancient western boxing are to be found in the first portion of books on the modern sport written by sportswriters, martial artists, and boxing critics. These are largely opinion pieces written by authors who are not disciplined researchers, and are often riddled with factual errors. This will be the case with any work that is strictly dependent on tertiary and secondary sources.

Source example #1:
   John F. Gilbey, *Western Boxing & World Wrestling: Story & Practice*, North Atlantic, Berkeley, CA, 1986, pages 12-17, 91
   This source is a veritable minefield of fallacy; Gilbey variously states the following, <u>all</u> of which are false: "…as time went on soft handwrapping became leather… They blocked punches with their left arms but knew little of slipping and ducking. Their blows were primarily hammering ones… Spartans did not engage in pugilism [pugmakhia] or the pancration… Only biting was forbidden… In the entire history of the Greek Olympics only two boxing champions, Theagenes [Theogenes] and Cleitomachus [Kleitomakhos] won both the boxing and the pancration in the same Olympics. Because the pancration did not permit the use of the gloves or cestus, the boxer was at a disadvantage… After Greece was conquered by Rome, the art degenerated into a Greco-Roman rivalry… The Romans introduced the cestus [caestus] and its extension the deadly myrmex "the limb piercer"… Theagenes [Theogenes] of Thasos who reportedly killed over one thousand eight hundred men… Perhaps the best grappler Rome ever produced was Melancomas…"

   Let me briefly address the above fallacies since Gilbey, although the author of various outrageous tall tales [his name isn't really John F. Gilbey either] is widely regarded by martial artists as an authority on boxing.
   1. The soft hand wraps *were* leather, and as time went on they became hard –or sharp.
   2. Slipping and ducking were highly regarded ancient boxing tactics.
   3. The hammerfist was a well-known but *not* a primary punch.
   4. At least 2 Olympic boxing champions were Spartans.
   5. Biting and gouging were prohibited in the pankration.
   6. Theogenes & Kleitomakhos both failed to win boxing & pankration at the same Olympic agon. There were at least 3 other champion boxer/pankratiast.

7. Pankratiasts were permitted hand protection but usually went bare-handed.
8. Greek prize-fighters of the Roman period unionized and cooperated with Roman Emperors who generally supported Greek athletes as model citizens.
9. Caestus was the Latin term for a composite boxing gauntlet consisting of glove, padding, soft straps, and hard or "sharp" straps.
10. Myrmex is the Greek term for ant, which was applied as a slang term to both soft and sharp wraps, which were both known to "bite" or cut, just as Mexican style boxing gloves are known for their "cutting" qualities in modern times.
11. Theogenes is not known to have killed a single opponent, and, in fact, won many of his victories bloodlessly via walk-over when opponents declined to fight him.
12. Not only was Melankomas a boxer and *not* a wrestler, he was notorious for his evasiveness and knack for avoiding contact totally—not even punching or clinching!

After this litany of opinionated book-born errors one could be forgiven for rushing to the nearest martial arts encyclopedia for more authoritative commentary on the martial arts of the West. However, these pieces are essentially articles written by magazine writers who are used to quickly utilizing secondary and tertiary sources.

Source example #2:

John Corcoran and Emil Farkas with Stuart Sobel. *The Original Martial Arts Encyclopedia: Tradition-History-Pioneers*, Pro-Action, Los Angeles, CA, 1993, page 117

Overall, the authors' attention to Greek boxing is superior to most, and their only errors are those perpetuated because of their use of Norman E. Gardiner as a primary source. Their entry on the pankration entertains an interesting fantasy about pankration spawning all Asian martial arts which I have addressed. Of course, modern boxing does not even deserve an entry in this vast tome. However, if a European decides to kick, he may be permitted to call himself a martial artist; so savate is covered in detail, for the most part with accuracy, until the authors attempt an interesting swipe at the crude fistic ritual of the hated West..... "The great John L. Sullivan was once staggered, and then knocked to the ground by the kicks of a savateur."

Actually, the great, fat, drunken, rude, and heavy-handed John L. never fought a savateur! So what might our karate writers be fantasizing about?

The Gods of Boxing

John L. did fight once on French soil to escape the attention of the British authorities. The bout was conducted in the rain and mud against a run-and-hug *English* middleweight by the name of Charlie Mitchell—Sullivan's old nemesis, who he referred to as "that bombastic sprinter!" During the course of this closely reported bout Mitchell raked Sullivan's shin with his three ½ inch cleats causing the great John L. to take a knee. Makes you wonder, doesn't it?

Surely though, a main-stream encyclopedia, with an ancient boxing entry written by the editor-and-chief of *The Ring* –the gosh-darn bible of modern boxing!—would give our fistic forefathers a fair shake?

Source example #3:

World Book Encyclopedia, B, Volume 2, 1988 Edition, Boxing entry by Nigel Collins, page 541

"Boxing was a brutal spectacle in ancient Greece. Two young men would sit on flat stones, face-to-face, with their fists wrapped in *thongs* [strips of leather]. At a signal they began to hit each other until one of them fell to the ground unconscious. The other man then continued to beat his opponent until he died."

Greek boxing was nothing like what is described above. The only accurate part of this entry was the description of the hand wraps. The author continues with a slightly more accurate description of boxing under the Romans only to finish with the following fallacy: "In the first century before Christ, they [the Romans] prohibited boxing completely."

In fact, boxing under the Romans continued to enjoy popular and official support from 300 B.C. until *at least* A.D. 384—not a bad run, aye? Most of the material written on ancient boxing consists of 1 to 3 paragraph entries found in the introduction to the numerous books on modern boxing. These entries invariably rely on the above source, or a series of poorly researched pieces that ultimately rely on the source below, which is as far back as I've been able to trace the fantasy of seated boxing death matches.

Source example #4:

Menke, Frank G. *The Encyclopedia of Sports*, A.S. Barnes, New York, 1953, pg. 233

Mr. Menke unfortunately confused the legend of Theseus—who, if he existed, lived between 1600 and 900 B.C.—and his seated boxers, with the career of Theogenes, which peaked in 476 B.C., and gladiatorial pugilism which was current around A.D. 200. He managed to mangle at least 1100 years of fistic history in a few sentences, and confuse the issue for generations of lazy sports-writers to come.

The Gods of Boxing

As for the legend of Theseus promoting seated boxing. If he did, he was a humanitarian, because the weak punches landed during a seated bench fight would at best topple his fighters onto the floor. The Athenians [Theseus was the legendary founder of Athens] were renowned seamen, and the latter renowned seamen of the British age of sail were known to conduct bare-knuckle bouts seated on their sea-chests, usually while drunk. My instinct is that the legend of Theseus' seated boxers is a description of a pirate Kings' rowdy dinner party.

Historical Novels: For the most part the only popular books that get anything right concerning ancient Greco-Roman martial arts are historical novels. These should be read primarily to understand the cultural landscape of the time.

Secondary Sources

Academic works that translate and interpret the ancient sources are priceless. Only a handful of scholars have ventured into the field of ancient athletics, and their rare works will be covered in the *Select Bibliography of Modern Sources in Order of Importance*.

Primary Sources

Although the ancient literature available for study is vast, it never-the-less consists of a fragmented mass of numerous genres of varied quality composed over many centuries. In some aspects later ancient authors possessed less knowledge than modern authors due to the lack of archaeological evidence—archaeology being a modern discipline. Also, the fact that most ancient literature did not survive, and that ancient authors tended to be conversant in the entire body of literature extant in their own day, reminds us that they possessed much knowledge not available to the modern scholar. These sources will be examined, chronologically. Many excellent sources, such as Cicero and Virgil, are not included In the *Select Bibliography of Ancient Sources*, found below.

The Author's Reading Method

Tertiary sources are read once, with few notes taken. Secondary sources are read between four and seven times with a highlighting pen. Primary sources are skimmed for key words, with pertinent passages notated and later reread from one to three times. The titles examined in this manner from September 1998 thru March 2005 total 1152 and were originally compiled as a 125 page bibliography, the publication of which would drive the price of the book up so far as to make it inaccessible to the average reader. Those titles referenced in footnotes in the text were read during the final composition of the book between April and November of 2005 as the manuscript was being reviewed by the readers. The following select bibliographies include only those titles which were indispensable in the formation and exposition of the author's thesis on ancient western boxing and related forms of prize-fighting.

All of the literary research was, in its final form, measured against the author's own experience as a fighter and coach. All physical reconstructions of ancient combat methods conducted for this study were non-choreographed, full-contact, *contests*.

Part Two: Select Bibliography of Modern Sources in Order of Importance

Of the many historians and novelists who have painted word pictures of the life of ancient Greece, those whose works were most indispensable to this author are properly credited below for reforming the past in this author's mind. Those few scholars who have ventured into the field of ancient athletics made the author's task of analyzing ancient Greek prize-fighting possible, where it would have been impossible without the insight provided by their scholarship. The first, most prolific, and most prominent is E. Norman Gardiner, an Englishman who published between 1910 and 1930. He wrote 4 volumes over this time period, essentially summarized in his final work, which, as of 2005, is currently available in the following edition.

#1 Gardiner, E, Norman. *Athletics in the Ancient World*, Dover, Mineola, NY, 2002, pages vii-238

Gardiner, throughout his various books, expresses an unusually deep understanding of boxing, which no modern academic could match, as college boys do precious little boxing these days. His historical work is also first rate.

The Gods of Boxing

Where you have to be suspicious of Gardiner is in the area of cultural prejudice: he loves the Greeks and detests the Romans. He is an early 20th century physical culturalist who hates small heads and big muscles and is deeply disturbed by the trend toward professionalism in sports, which was beginning in his day and continues to boom in ours. To read Gardiner insightfully you have to read a lot of stuff written by dead white 19th century elitists to know where he was coming from.

#2 Poliakoff, Michael, B. *Combat Sports in the Ancient World: Competition, Violence and Culture,* Yale, New Hanen, CT, 1987, pages ix-191

Professor Poliakoff offers all the best insights that modern academics can draw from the rich agonistic culture of ancient Greece. Little morsels, like how to read art based on the limitations of the media, are priceless. He also demonstrates a keen understanding of ancient wrestling based on some kind of exposure to modern college-level competition. His only real drawback is a lack of boxing knowledge, which we really can't expect him to possess, since he does think for a living, and being punched in the head is not exactly a pursuit compatible with the highest levels of academic achievement. What Poliakoff does at his best is to put the ancient sources in context, and point out avenues for exploring the ancient experience with an ancient perspective. Of prime interest are the notes to the illustrations prior to the acknowledgements and the appendix and notes following the text.

#3 Burckhardt, Jacob. *The Greeks and Greek Civilization*, St. Martin's Press, NY, 1998, pages 1x-427.

This academic giant of the 19th Century was a successful art critic who actually suppressed his own book on Greek civilization during his lifetime for fear of his views on the then romanticized Greeks negatively effecting his academic esteem. For this very reason Burckhardt's work is the only one of his age to stand the test of time. It remains the standard by which other studies of ancient Greek life must be judged. Burckhardt's accomplishment reminds us that there is no substitute for insight.

#4 Finley, M. I. *The World of Odysseus*, The Folio Society, London, 2002, pages xi-186

Originally published in1954, Finley's work is a shining example of mid 20th Century history, as opposed to late 20th century historiography. Despite the fact that he was a socialist Finley presents a balanced view of ancient life free of his own beliefs. This work is a masterpiece of scholarship in its purest form.

#5 Wolfe, Gene. *Latro in the Mist*, Orb, NY, 2003, pages 13-639

This is actually a re-issuing of two fantasy/historical-fiction novels by the best sci-fi fantasy author of the late 20th Century. This is some of the best first-person fiction of any kind ever written, demonstrating keen insights into the world of the fighting man and the cultural life of ancient Hellas as well. Wolfe was a Korean War combat veteran, and his experience obviously informs the worldview of his protagonist Latro, a Roman mercenary. The ancient author who most inspired Wolfe was Xenophon, an Athenian mercenary captain and historian.

#6 Golden, Mark. *Sport and Society in Ancient Greece*, Cambridge, NY, 1998, pages ix-185

This is an excellent example of athletic anthropology. It's not an easy read, but is densely textured and well worth re-reading.

#7 Miller, Stephen G. *Arete: Greek Sports from Ancient Sources*, University of California Press, Berkeley, CA, 1991, pages vii-227

This is simply a mass of translations accompanied by contextual introductions by the editor, who is sufficiently knowledgeable to provide priceless commentaries.

#8 Larmour, David H. J. *Stage and Stadium: Drama and Athletics in Ancient Greece*, Weidmann, Hildesheim, Germany, 1999, pages 1-192

Some of the best ancient studies are only available in German. Finding an English translation of a German work always rated as a lucky find in my quest.

#9 Kyle, Donald G. *Athletics in Ancient Athens*, E. J. Brill, Leiden, The Netherlands, 1987, pages 1-228

Outside of archaeological finds Athens provides us with the bulk of our knowledge concerning the typical athlete of the age. Of course, Athens was no typical town.

#10 Spivey, Nigel. *The Ancient Olympics: A History*, Oxford, NY, 2004, pages xv-263

This is the most recent and most readable of the scholarly works on ancient Greek athletics.

#11 Davis, Victor Hanson. *The Wars of the Ancient Greeks*, Cassell, London, 1999, pages 8-218

Hanson is the foremost expert on ancient Greek warfare, his work is therefore indispensable to anyone examining war-related arts of the period. A good read.

#12 Bury, J. B. *A History of Greece to the Death of Alexander [Fourth Edition]*, St. Martins, London, 1989, pages

The fact that this book has been reprinted 48 times since its original publication in 1900, with only three archaeological updates to the text, speaks well for J.B. Bury as an historian. This author utilized Bury as a standard for evaluating the works of others. The chronological nature of his work is its greatest strength.

#13 Grant, Michael. *The Founders of the Western World: A History of Greece and Rome*, Scribner's, NY, 1991, pages 1-121

Grant is the most respected general historian of ancient Greece and Rome. Accessing his contributions is always a rewarding effort.

#14 Cox, William D. *Boxing in Art and Literature*. Reynal & Hitchcock, NY, 1935, pages 1-33

Cox presents a priceless anthology of boxing literature and artwork.

#15 Ross, Stewart. *The Original Olympic Games*, Peter Bedrick Books, Lincolnwood, IL, 1996, pages 1-47

Ross' work is a shining example of how brief sketches intended to educate children often serve as better secondary sources on ancient subjects than general works intended for the modern adult reader.

#16 Cartledge, Paul. *Spartan Reflections*, University of California Press, Berkeley, CA, 2001, pages ix-230

This book is another example of modern historiography at its indecisive best. The ability of modern academics to restructure history by way of argument is both disconcerting and necessary; a reminder that history means inquiry, and, that strict rules of inquiry, may often yield answers that simply beg an unanswerable question…

#17 Cunliffe, Barry. *The Extraordinary Journey of Pytheas the Greek*, Walker & Company, NY, 2002, pages vii-178

One of the few works to focus on Magna Graecia, is this reconstruction of the Westward explorations of a contemporary of Alexander. The most important aspect of Cunliffe's work is his demonstration of how to sift through the rubble of ancient literature in the quest for a plausible foundation for the fragmented stories which have reached us through the ages.

Select Bibliography of Ancient Sources in Chronological Order

All of the specific boxing references found in the literature from the period under study have been cited within the text. The following bibliography is a chronological review of all the ancient works which provided direct or contextual insights to the life of the ancient Greek prize-fighter. All of the entries below provide indispensable insights into the social and cultural context that informed the life of the ancient Greek prize-fighter, and should be read in their entirety. Those sources that provided direct mention of prize-fighting activities are indicated by an.* Sources that post-date the period of this study have only been included when the authors of these texts of the Hellenistic and Roman period have directly addressed the subject of prize-fighting in the Heroic-Archaic and Classical periods, as prose, poetry or commentary. Dates are approximate, and meant to indicate the probable apex or median point of the author's literary activity.

    750 to 720 B.C.: Homer, *The Iliad*, The Odyssey**
        Hesiod, *Works and Days, Theogony*
    690 B.C.: Arkhilokhus, lyric poems
    680 B.C.: Tyrtaeus, *Warsongs**
    650 B.C.: Sappho, *Odes*
    620 B.C.: Alkaeus, *fragments*
      Alkman, *Parthenia*
    544 B.C.: Theognis, *Elegies*
    540 B.C.: Hipponax, *Testimonia*
      Aesop, *Fables*

Gerber, Douglas, E. *Greek Iambic Poetry: From the Seventh to Fifth Centuries B.C.*, Harvard, Cambridge, MA, 1999, pages 381, 437, 519

    490 B.C.: Simonides, *Epigrams*, Odes*
    484 B.C.: Aeskhylus, *The Persians, The Supplicants, Prometheus Bound, Seven Against Thebes*, Agamemnon, Khoephoroe, Eumenides**

The Gods of Boxing

476 B.C.: Pindar, *Olympian Odes*, Pythian Odes*, Isthmian Odes*, Nemean Odes**

465 B.C.: Bakhylides, *Odes & Epigrams**

441 B.C.: Sophokles, *Ajax and Antigone, Elektra, Oedipus Tyrannus, Trakhiniae**

434 B.C.: Herodotus, *Histories*

430 B.C.: Euripides, *Iphigeneia in Taurika*, Alkestis*, Fury of Herakles, Children of Herakles, Phoenician Maidens, Medea, Alexander, Prologus*

412 B.C.: Aristophanes, *Clouds, Wasps, Peace, Birds, Frogs, Eating Soldiers' Bread**

406 B.C.: Thukydides, *History of the Peloponnesian War*

Paton, W. R. *The Greek Anthology*, Putnam, NY, 1917: Volume II, pages 53, 139, 237, 285, 376; Volume III, pages 301, 447, 588; Volume IV, pages 6, 36, 75-81, 112, 129, 161, 351; Voulume V, pages 23, 25, 52, 55, 94, 96, 97, 105, 186, 335-87

400 B.C.: Hippokrates: *On Wounds in the Head*, On Factures, On Joints, Instruments of Reduction, Nature of Man, Regimen in Health, Nutriment*, Ancient Medicine*

Lysias, *Against Eratosthenes*

380 B.C.: Isokrates, *Antidosis*, To Demonikus, To Nikokles, Panegyrikus, To Philip, Arkhidamus, Against Kallimakhus, Aeginetikus, Against Lokhites, To Antipitar, To Timotheus, To the Rulers of Mytilene, Areopagitikus, Panathenaikus, Evagoras, Hellen, Busiris, The Team of Horses, Trapezitikus*

Xenophon, *Helleniks*, Anabasis*, Memorabilia*, Skripta Minora*, Encomium of Agesilaus*, Hipparkhikus, Kynegetikus, Oekonomikus, Kyropaedeia*

Plato, *Lakhes, Gorgias*, Protagoras, Euthydemus, Kratylus, Alkibiades II*, Republic*, Philebus*, Laws*, Theaetetus, Sophist, Statesman, Timaeus, Kleinias and the Athenian**

350 B.C.: Onasander, *The Strategist*

Aeneas, *On the Defense of Fortifications*

Asklepiodotus, *Tactics*

336 B.C.: Demosthenes, *On the Peace, Against Meidias, Against Aristokrates, The Funeral Speech, The Erotic Essay*, Second Phillipik**

Aeskhines, *Against Timarkhos, Against Ktesiphon*

330 B.C.: Aristotle, *Nikomakhaen Ethics*, Categories, Physics, Politics*

320 B.C.: Theophrastus, *Areskeia*, Lalia*, Anaisthesia*, Opsimathia**

Menander, *The Arbitrants, The Counterfeit Herakles, Aspis, Dyskolos*, Enkheiridion, Epitrepontes**

183

275 B.C.: Theokritus, *Hymn to the Dioskuri*, The Herdsman*, The Little Herakles*, Thyrsis the Shepard and the Goatherd, Upon Arkhilochus, Upon Pisander, Life to be Enjoyed, Beauty*

    Moskhus, *Idylls*

    Epiktetus, *Handbook*

    Timokles, *The Boxer**

250 B.C.: Herondas, *The Matchmaker, The Whorehouse Manager, The Shoemaker, The Dream, Molpinos*

    Kallimakhus, *Aetia, Iambi, Hekale, Fragments**

    Strato, Meleager & Automedon, *Erotic Epigrams**

    Hierokles to Zenon, *Letters**

150 B.C.: Polybius, *History [Book 27.9, Position of Perseus in Greece]**

50 B.C.: Nepos, Cornelius, *Great Generals of Foreign Nations*

    Dionysius of Halikarnassus, *A History of Rome*

    Diodorus Siculus, *Histories**

A.D. 10: Strabo, *Geography**

A.D. 29: Valerius, Maximus. *Memorable Doings and Sayings**

    Phaedrus, *The Poet*

    Babrius, *The Fighting Cock*, Herakles and the Ox-driver*, Hero-cult*

A.D. 50: Curtius, Rufus Quintus, *Alexander the Great**

A.D.100: Plutarch, *Lives, Moralia,*

A.D. 120: Phlegon of Tralles, *Book of Marvels*

A.D. 150: Diogenes Laertius, *Lives of the Greek Philosophers**

A.D. 170: Pausanias, *Description of Greece**

A.D. 180: Alkiphron, *letters*

A.D. 190: Athenaeus, *Banquet of the Learned**

A.D. 225: Philsostratus. *On the Naked Exercises*, Love Letters to a Boy*

[Yes, you read that title correctly. I read this from a rare copy at the Peabody Conservatory, where the head librarian—an elderly women who could read 7 languages, and did not trust me around the nubile student body and the female staff—was in the habit of looking over my shoulder as I read. If she had seen me reading this she probably would have warned the janitor to stay away from me. I read this piece in a hurry and did not come back for seconds.]

    A.D.250: Philostratus the Lemnian, *Pictures in a Gallery**

    A.D. 400: Quintus Smyrnaeus, *The Fall of Troy**

    A.D. 450: Macrobius, *Saturnalia*